"Cannoneers, To Your Posts!"

James H. Cooper's Battery B, First Pennsylvania Light Artillery at Gettysburg

*"The honors and the glories of
duties well and faithfully performed"*

*To Bob with my compliments
thank-you for your interest
Frank J Piatek
29th April 2007*

by Frank J. Piatek

Library of Congress Control Number: 2006925968

ISBN-13: 978-0-9760563-6-2
ISBN-10: 0-9760563-6-4

Printed by

MECHLING
BOOKBINDERY

1124 Oneida Valley Road - Rt. 38
Chicora, PA 16025-3820
1-800-941-3735
www.mechlingbooks.com

TABLE OF CONTENTS

Members of Cooper's Battery B at Gettysburg

PREFACE

The quest for historical truth is filled with pitfalls. The evidence to be used in that quest is often contradictory, incomplete, or might not even exist, leaving much to conjecture. This is the dilemma of the historian who looks for answers to certain questions to ascertain truth. While technology may help us reevaluate the tangible evidence we already have in a new or different way, the raw material itself is either there or it is not.

Science concerns itself with reoccurring phenomena that are capable of being constantly viewed and reevaluated—each time more fully as technology evolves to permit it. That is not true in the quest for historical truth because the event cannot be played back exactly as it happened to allow us a second look. It is ephemeral. Only vestiges of it remain. All the historian can hope for is to find those vestiges of the past that were locked away from others before him.

Throughout my presentation, the reader will find references to contradictory renditions of events from different perspectives. That might be disturbing for those looking for what actually occurred. For them, the evidence must be internally consistent and also be compatible with physical facts and reason so that they can be satisfied that truth has been served. But if that is what is necessary for the reader here, then perhaps I have not accomplished that goal any better than others before me by still leaving more questions than answers. To resolve all the inconsistencies is too difficult a task for any one person and may, in fact, be an impossible burden to successfully carry out anyway, given the physical and personal limitations under which individual historians operate. Rather it is my purpose to stimulate readers to carry on the search for truth themselves. After all, there is always a greater likelihood of success in ascertaining the truth when there are many of us looking for it. To that extent, my present wish is that after reading the history of the battery's service at Gettysburg, the readers will go on to try to resolve some of the contradictions or to find the missing parts of the puzzle that eluded me. In the process, perhaps they, too, can truly understand and appreciate how difficult the quest really is.

In researching this book, I had the pleasure of visiting the United States Military History Institute, Ridgway Hall, in Carlisle, Pennsylvania in the summer of 2005. At the conclusion of my research there, I was informed that a special display entitled "Soldier in the Attic" could be viewed upstairs. The presentation involved military artifacts that might be found in anyone's attic dealing with any period in our history, tangible items which might provide answers to someone's queries, now or perhaps in the future. The implication for me was that such items should not be destroyed because they might serve as part of the mosaic. But how many of us today, in our disposable society with a limited perspective of the relevance of anything that does not immediately affect us personally, simply discard these vestiges of the past? They may be uniforms, letters, diaries, journals, or photographs of people, places, or events—any one of which can assist historians in resolving questions of fact.

Perhaps after one reads this book, a spark of curiosity will cause the individual to search out any vestiges of the past in his/her possession and control that could help complete the mosaic. If that occurs, then I have been successful.

The focus of this study is, obviously, on James H. Cooper's Battery B, First Pennsylvania Light Artillery. But readers will note that, when applicable, I have included a discussion of the infantry units supporting the battery as well as the service of other batteries which were part of the operations. This is necessary because individual units do not fight in isolation in the first place, and one can only appreciate what occurred in the context of the total strategy. By the same token, I have not dwelled on things that were far removed from the battery's experience at Gettysburg or might complicate the story. That is beyond the scope of what this book is about. Of necessity, I had to exercise some selectivity and fully expect that some will think the study too thin or too detailed in certain particulars, depending on their own predilections or expectations. Much of the detail, including conflicting accounts of the action, have been relegated to explanatory endnotes so as not to unduly disturb the flow of the narrative.

Frank J. Piatek

ACKNOWLEDGMENTS

Most of the material about Cooper's Battery can be found at The Pennsylvania State Archives in Harrisburg, Pennsylvania. That along with other primary sources such as the Official Records, Colonel Wainwright's journal, and James A. Gardner's letters to Colonel Bachelder and others regarding the battery's placement and operations have been relied upon. The recollections of James P. Alcorn, one of the members of the battery, was a fortuitous find at the Gettysburg National Military Park Library.

I have not neglected citing secondary sources by eminent historians for several reasons: First, like an expert witness in a trial who can evaluate the facts of a specific case and offer an expert opinion even though he did not actually witness the event, so too the professional historians, as a result of their broad study of the campaign, can add an interpretation that plain reliance on cold facts alone would not. Second, the use of established secondary sources provides a benchmark to evaluate primary source material that may be contradictory. In some cases, even the experts may disagree and so it is interesting to evaluate their respective treatments of the same event. In other cases, they may agree which provides corroboration for what is being discussed. Third, in some cases it is more succinct to have a secondary source synthesize certain accepted primary sources than to make the present study more cumbersome by string citing them all over again.

In researching this project, I have met many people along the way who have been most gracious of their time to assist me. Battery B was organized in Lawrence County, Pennsylvania where I reside, but ironically there was really not that much information available locally at my disposal. To the extent that there was, however, I was able to ferret it out with the help of Beverly Zona in the historical reference room at the Lawrence County Public Library. Bev has an interest in local history and had served as Executive Director of the Lawrence County Historical Society when I met her as a Board member years ago. Current director, Robert Presnar, provided me the opportunity to view the post-war glass plate image of Cooper which is in the archives of the Society.

Dwight Copper at the McGill Library, Westminster College in New Wilmington, Pennsylvania provided some copies of newspaper clippings as well as his research involving the old Methodist Church Cemetery where some of the members of the battery are interred. Certainly, my appreciation must go to Kenneth C. Turner of Ellwood City, Pennsylvania who kindly shared some images of battery members from his collection of Civil War photographs. In addition, Emily Hoffman granted permission for me to use a post-war photograph of Cooper in her possession, as did Nancy Gardner to use one depicting the veterans of the battery at one of their reunions. Those images have been reproduced in this book. Hal Jespersen has made Civil War maps for Wikipedia, the free on-line encyclopedia, that are available to the public and are valuable for their simplicity in depicting the flow of the battle for the average reader. Wikipedia is subject to input by many contributors who can modify existing information for better or worse. The renditions of Jespersen's maps I have used here, in my opinion, are a fairly good representation of the action.

John Heiser at the Gettysburg National Military Park Library was accommodating during my visit there as was Beth Trescott at the battlefield's Archive Office. Dean Knudsen, Park Curator, was helpful in clearing up some questions about the first monument to the battery erected on East Cemetery Hill in the 1880's. Sarah R. Fuss of the Trinity United Church of Christ in Gettysburg confirmed some burial details of one of the members of the battery. The personnel at the Pennsylvania State Archives in Harrisburg and the United States Army Military History Institute, Ridgway Hall, in Carlisle, Pennsylvania spared nothing to ensure that I was able to obtain the information I needed and made my experience obtaining it pleasurable. Joan K. Weaver, Director of the Kinsley Public Library in Kinsley, Kansas, provided me with some interesting postwar biographical information about James P. Alcorn from its records.

Perhaps one of the most interesting discoveries was a descendent of the Alcorn family who had supplied the transcription of her ancestor's reminiscences about the Gettysburg campaign years ago. Originally sent to Pamplin Park Civil War Site in Virginia, the transcription eventually came to repose at the Gettysburg National Military Park Library. Although I had some doubts that I would ever locate this person after the passage of time, my efforts were fruitful. Her name is Ada-Marie Bowers of Santa Barbara, California. While we have never met personally except through correspondence and a telephone communication, Ms. Bowers was as cordial and accommodating as one could possibly expect in helping me with my efforts. She provided me with a pre-war portrait of the Alcorn family that I have included.

The reader should also be aware that I do not write the history of Battery B at Gettysburg under the mantle "professional historian." But like so many others who have a passion for history and enjoy searching for the truth, I have undertaken this project as my first effort. My interest in the Civil War was spawned over 50 years ago when, as a child, I read McKinley Kantor's Gettysburg[1] which was but one book in a juvenile series dealing with different epochs of our history. From that, my parents arranged many vacation trips for us to visit the battlefield, and the rest, as one might say, is history. To them I owe my gratitude for putting up with those sojourns just to please me.

It was that interest which also led to my meeting my future wife, Mary. Being from Hanover, Pennsylvania which is close to Gettysburg, Mary would not only share trips with me to the battlefield, but her parents and other family members were also very kind in allowing us to stay with them as I toured it myself for days at a time. Needless to say, I encouraged Mary to visit with her parents as much as she liked with the expectation, of course, that I would tag along so that I could tramp the field. As a good friend and wonderful wife, she was perceptive enough to see how much my interest in Civil War history was a part of my life and did not try to take that away from me. Her appreciation of my passion and her encouragement for me to write this book must certainly be acknowledged.

Finally, I cannot leave out some of the most friendly people anyone could ever meet who share a common interest in the Civil War. These include the members of the Mahoning Valley Civil War Roundtable in Youngstown, Ohio, particularly Hugh Earnhart, former Professor of History and Chairman of the Department at Youngstown University, now retired, who had originally established the organization. The people there have provided the intellectual stimulation for me to consider doing this project. Also included are countless friends from reenacting groups who keep the spirit and enthusiasm alive for all of us and with whom I have shared a personal bond over many years. My thanks to all.

Notes

[1] McKinley Kantor, Gettysburg, (New York: Random House, 1952). This was part of the Landmark Series of American history books for younger children.

INTRODUCTION

"Captain Cooper, you are the bravest man in the army!" It was December 13, 1862, and the place was an open plain south of Fredericksburg, Virginia where the Pennsylvania Reserves had made a momentary breakthrough in the Confederate lines. The Reserves came tumbling back, being unable to exploit their success for lack of reinforcements, with the enemy on their heels. It was the only success the Federals had that day, but it was fleeting at best.

Standing resolute at their positions were the men of James H. Cooper's Battery B, First Pennsylvania Light Artillery watching as the Reserves made their withdrawal. It was pay-back time for the efforts the 9th Reserves made in re-capturing Cooper's guns five months earlier at the Battle of Glendale, and the battery captain would not let them down. Cooper's men, with other batteries alongside, waited. The enemy approached to within 75 yards. As it wheeled left, a brigade of Georgians made a perfect target for the cannoneers to fire into its weakened right flank, and Cooper did not hesitate.

Belching forth double rounds of canister, his guns along with others stopped the Confederate counter-attack in its tracks. One staff officer said that the artillery "opened with a vigor I have never seen sur-passed." Another officer said that the field was covered with "Rebel dead and dying, heads off, legs off, and arms." He characterized the work as slaughter.[1]

Cooper's efforts did not go unnoticed by First Corps commander Major General John F. Reynolds on this occasion. It was he who complimented the twenty-two year old battery commander on his bravery as he saw what took place. Almost seven months later, Cooper and his battery of four guns, which was really reduced to three at times, would occupy five different positions on the field at Gettysburg and expend 1,050 rounds of ammunition. At war's end, it would have the reputation of sustaining the highest battle-related deaths of any volunteer light artillery battery in the Federal army.[2] Unfortunately, Reynolds who was commanding the left wing of the army at Gettysburg would never see a repeat performance of Cooper's bravery there, or anywhere else for that matter. Before Cooper's artillerymen could even unlimber their guns at Gettysburg, Reynolds would be dead.

Organized at Mount Jackson, Lawrence County, Pennsylvania on April 26, 1861, and known as the Mount Jackson Guards, Battery B (43rd Regiment) was originally attached to McCall's Division of the Pennsylvania Reserves. It had the distinction of participating in the first victory of the Army of the Potomac at Dranesville, Virginia on December 20, 1861. Thereafter, it participated in 24 other engagements, in-cluding the Seven Days battles, Second Manassas, South Mountain, Antietam, Fredericksburg, Chancellorsville, Gettysburg, Mine Run, U.S. Grant's Overland Campaign battles, and actions around Petersburg, Virginia before concluding service after Appomattox.[3] Its first captain was Henry T. Danforth, a veteran of the Mexican War, who was promoted to lieutenant colonel and assigned elsewhere. Danforth, wanting to remain with the battery, resigned his commission and enlisted again, this time under Cooper. He was killed during the Seven Days battles at Glendale.[4]

The unit was composed of farmer's sons, businessmen, and schoolteachers, "all in the prime and vigor of manhood; from a locality unexcelled in thrift and in the intelligence and religious culture of its inhabitants."[5] One of these young men was James P. Alcorn who, with his brother Alexander, joined early in 1861. Both had been students and lived in Enon Valley near Mount Jackson. As all the men marched to the train depot in Enon Valley to leave, they were met along the way by farmers who hitched horses to wagons so that they could ride. By October 12 of that year James became a sergeant. His brother remained a private. James had the distinction of firing one of the first guns across the Potomac River in defense of Washington and was later wounded at Glendale and Second Manassas.[6]

*Captain James Harvey Cooper
(Courtesy of Kenneth C. Turner)*

Cooper's Battery, or Battery B as it was commonly known, had participated in some of the hardest fighting encountered by the Army of the Potomac, and like the infantry and cavalry branches, had suffered from poor leadership at the top. On June 28, 1863, another officer, Major General George G. Meade, would take his turn.[7] A Pennsylvanian although born in Cadiz, Spain to American parents, Meade was already known to Cooper and the Pennsylvania Reserves. Meade commanded the Reserves at Fredericksburg following in the footsteps of Reynolds who had commanded them at the Battle of Second Manassas. At the time of this assignment, he was commanding the Fifth Corps while it and the rest of the Federal army were following the enemy's movement northward. Although the exact intentions of Confederate General Robert E. Lee and his Army of Northern Virginia were not known, it was obvious that an invasion of the North was happening based on the presence of Lee's advance elements in Pennsylvania. The opposing armies would meet in just three days on the outskirts of a small town called Gettysburg where Meade would be put to the test. For many who knew him, Meade was a no-nonsense individual with a caustic personality. Thoroughly competent, the new commander of the Army of the Potomac had two problems facing him on the eve of a new battle: he had to coalesce his scattered army corps quickly to meet Lee's army once he was able to locate it and simultaneously devise a winning strategy in short order.

Notes

[1] From Francis A. O'Reilly, The Fredericksburg Campaign, Winter War on the Rappahannock (Baton Rouge: Louisiana State University Press, 2003), pp. 230-231. Used by permission of the publisher. O'Reilly's rendition is perhaps the best tactical study of that campaign available today. For an excellent tactical study of the Seven Days battles, including Glendale (Charles City Crossroads), see Brian K. Burton, Extraordinary Circumstances, the Seven Days Battles, (Bloomington, Indiana: Indiana University Press, 2001).

[2] The War of the Rebellion: A Compilation of the Official Records of the Union and Confederate Armies, Series I, Vol. 27, Part 1 [hereinafter referred to as O.R. Vol. 27.1] (Washington, D.C.: Government Printing Office, 1889), p. 365. William F. Fox, Regimental Losses in the American Civil War, (Dayton, Ohio: Morningside Press, 1985), p. 7. Fox states that the battery lost 21 officers and men killed or mortally wounded. During its existence, the battery fired over 11,200 rounds. Samuel P. Bates, History of the Pennsylvania Volunteers, Vol. 1, (Harrisburg: B. Singerly, State Printer 1870), p. 952.

[3] See listing on Battery B's monument on East Cemetery Hill, Gettysburg, PA. Also see: Col. John P. Nicholson, Pennsylvania at Gettysburg, Vol. II (Harrisburg: E.K. Myers, State Printer,1893), pp. 874-886 and Bates, History of the Pennsylvania Volunteers, Vol. 1, pp. 947-952. The battery had a full four years of service. There are photographs taken of the battery in Petersburg which appear in Francis T. Miller (ed.), The Photographic History of the Civil War, (New York: Review of Reviews Co., 1911), Vol. 1, pp. 22-23 and Vol. 3, pp. 176-179. One shows photographer Matthew Brady standing behind

Cooper. For an excellent discussion and critique of these photographs, including the manner in which they were taken, see William A. Frassanito's Grant and Lee, the Virginia Campaigns 1864-1865 (New York: Chas. Scribner's Sons, 1983), pp. 242-248.

4 Nicholson, p. 876; Donald W. Fox (ed.), Bridges to the Past, a Pictorial History of Lawrence County (State College, Pennsylvania: Commercial Printing, Inc., 1994), p. 122. Fairfax Downey in his The Guns of Gettysburg (New York: David McKay Company, Inc., 1958), pp. 34-35, erroneously states that Danforth was at Gettysburg.

5 Nicholson, p. 876.

6 Descriptive Roll of Officers and Men, 1861-1865, Series #18M.17, PA State Archives, Harrisburg, PA; James had attended Beaver Academy. Obituary, "Death Reaps Large Harvest," Kinsley Graphic, January 20, 1911. The obituary refers to him being wounded at those battles, but the annotation in the roster found in Bates' History of the Pennsylvania Volunteers does not so indicate. The reference to the men being picked up by farmers in wagons when entraining at Enon Valley is from the History of the Family of James Fullerton and Margaret Sharp, privately published [n.d.], p. 100, courtesy of Nancy Gardner a descendent of John M. Fullerton.

7 Meade replaced Major General Joseph Hooker who had commanded the army at the Battle of Chancellorsville nearly two months earlier. As Hooker's army followed Robert E. Lee's Army of Northern Virginia, Hooker asked to be relieved of command due to a disagreement with the Lincoln administration. Meade, who really never sought overall command nor even wanted it once presented, had to accept it because it was a direct order from the administration.

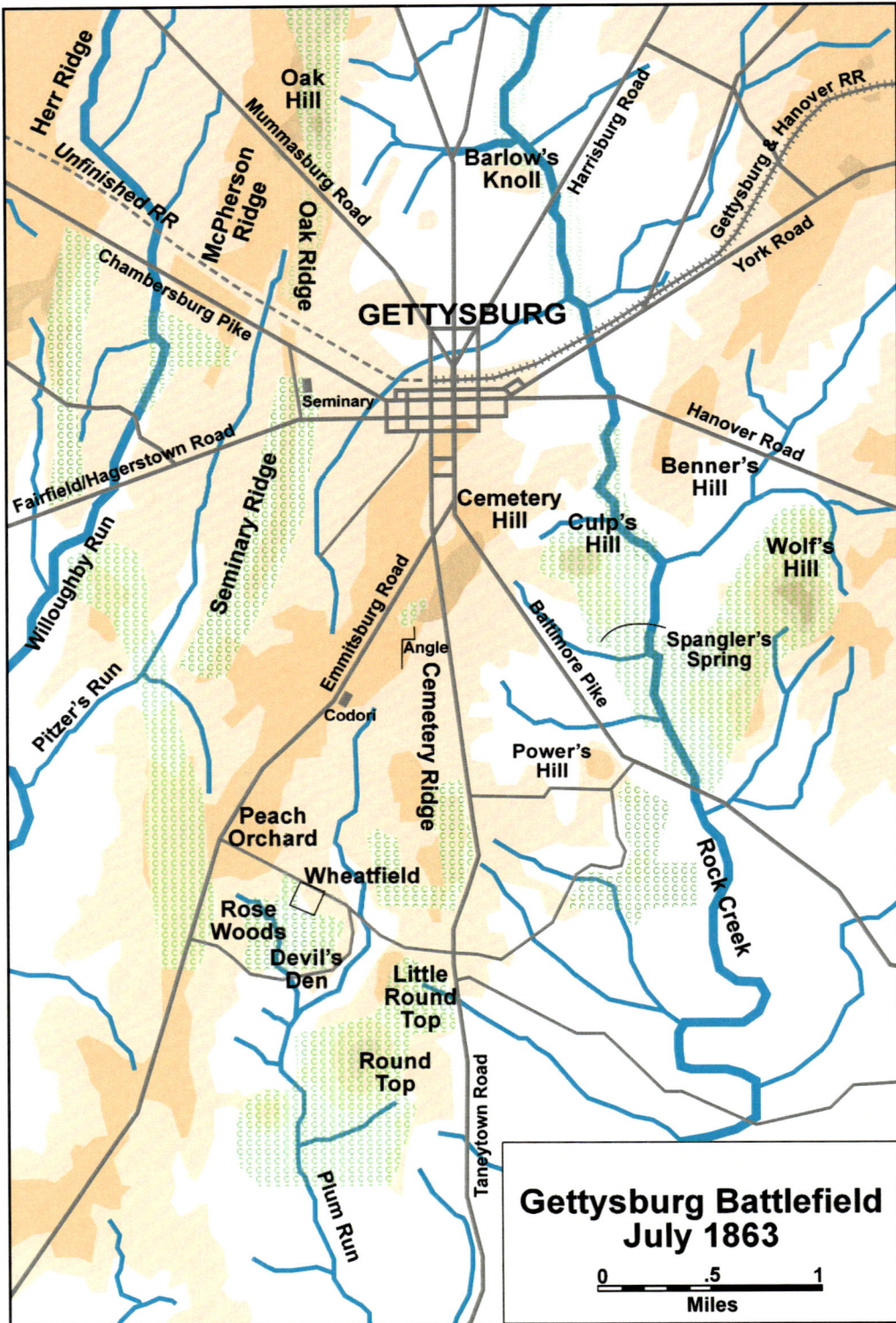

Herr Ridge
Oak Hill
Unfinished RR
Chambersburg Pike
McPherson Ridge
Mummasburg Road
Oak Ridge
Barlow's Knoll
Harrisburg Road
Gettysburg & Hanover RR
York Road
GETTYSBURG
Seminary
Fairfield/Hagerstown Road
Seminary Ridge
Hanover Road
Benner's Hill
Cemetery Hill
Culp's Hill
Wolf's Hill
Willoughby Run
Pitzer's Run
Emmitsburg Road
Angle
Codori
Cemetery Ridge
Baltimore Pike
Spangler's Spring
Power's Hill
Peach Orchard
Wheatfield
Rose Woods
Devil's Den
Little Round Top
Round Top
Rock Creek
Taneytown Road
Plum Run

Gettysburg Battlefield July 1863

0   .5   1
Miles

(Map courtesy of Hal Jespersen's Wikipedia Civil War Maps)

THE BATTLE AND AFTERWARD
GETTYSBURG—DAY ONE

The first brigade of Brigadier General Thomas A. Rowley's Third Division of the Federal First Corps was winding its way north toward the sound of battle near Gettysburg, Pennsylvania. It was covering the left flank of the army and approaches from Fairfield and Cashtown.[1] Crossing Sachs Bridge over Marsh Creek, it followed the Black Horse Tavern Road and the western bank of Willoughby Run toward the outskirts of the town. Composed of the 80th New York (20th Militia) and the 121st, 142nd, and 151st Pennsylvania, the brigade was now under the command of Colonel Chapman Biddle.

Attached to the entire First Corps was the artillery brigade under Colonel Charles S. Wainwright which consisted of the guns of Captain James A. Hall's 2nd Maine, Captain Greenleaf T. Stevens' 5th Maine, Captain Gilbert H. Reynolds' 1st New York Battery L, Lieutenant James Stewart's 4th U.S. Battery B, and Captain James H. Cooper's 1st Pennsylvania Battery B. All of these artillery units eventually figured into the ability of Federals to hold the Confederates at bay for a long period of time, trying to help fulfill General Reynolds' promise to Meade that he would fight the enemy "…inch by inch, and if driven into the town I will barricade the streets, and hold him back as long as possible."[2] Cooper's battery would play a large role in that effort on this day.

The battle was already underway when Biddle's men, accompanied by Cooper's battery, approached the field near the Fairfield (Hagerstown) Road. Earlier, Hall's battery had been engaged along with Brigadier General James S. Wadsworth's Division of the First Corps in relief of Brigadier General John Buford's First Division of Federal cavalry and Lieutenant John Calef's horse battery. Buford had met the Confederates as they plodded toward Gettysburg west of town, and the engagement evolved into a full-scale encounter with the First Corps infantry coming up in support. General Reynolds had been moving a portion of the famed Iron Brigade infantry into Herbst Woods south of the Chambersburg Pike. Just then he was instantly killed at the edge of the woodlot. Major General Abner Doubleday assumed command, someone who Wainwright thought was a "weak reed to lean upon."[3] The time was approximately 11:30 a.m.[4]

Colonel Charles S. Wainwright (Photograph from the Roger D. Hunt Collection, U.S. Army Military History Institute, Carlisle, Pennsylvania)

Biddle's brigade followed a circuitous route to reach the Federal position. Three parallel ridges running north and south flanked the area that his men encountered once they came upon the Fairfield Road. The Confederate reserve artillery battalion under Major William J. Pegram located on Herr Ridge to the west had been punishing the First Corps that morning, and both Calef and Hall had a hard time in dealing with his fire. Now Confederate Major D. G. McIntosh's artillery battalion would be added which would create even more problems for them. To Biddle's right and northeast of them was Herbst Woods occupied by Brigadier General Solomon Meredith's Iron Brigade, composed of Midwesterners who wore distinctive black hats. The Iron Brigade had been fighting in close combat with Confederate infantry ever since Reynolds led them in.[5]

A ridge extended from the Chambersburg Pike north of the woodlot and continued south toward the Fairfield Road. This was known as McPherson Ridge. The eastern portion of that ridge ran along the eastern border of the woodlot south toward the road. Although Biddle's men perhaps could not see it from their vantage point due to the trees, the western portion of the ridge entered the northern part of Herbst Woods. In between the two ridgelines north of the woodlot was a swale. Nearby stood the McPherson farm buildings. Finally, further to the east toward the town was yet another parallel ridge running north and south where the Lutheran Theological Seminary buildings were located. This was known as Seminary Ridge, and it extended south well beyond the Seminary. In between McPherson and Seminary Ridges was a meadow bordered by the Chambersburg Pike on the north and the Fairfield Road to the south. This area later became a killing field for the Confederates.

When he reached the Fairfield Road, Biddle placed his men into battle formation, faced north, and proceeded about 300 yards toward Herr Ridge before facing by the right flank to go east toward the Seminary, crossing Willoughby Run. Had he continued northward, Biddle would have struck the right flank of the Confederate line. But not realizing the strength of the enemy whose fire he drew, Biddle went looking for the rest of the First Corps.[6] The brigade eventually made its way to the crest of the eastern part of McPherson Ridge south of Herbst Woods and faced west toward the Confederate artillery on Herr Ridge. After an abortive advance in that direction toward Confederate skirmishers, it returned and sheltered itself somewhat by staying on the ridge's eastern slope (except for the 80th New York which remained on the crest).[7] Biddle's position extended the Federal line to the Fairfield Road, being the left flank of the First Corps. On the crest, facing west and positioned between the 80th New York and the 142nd Pennsylvania stood Cooper's guns, consisting of four 3-inch ordinance rifle pieces.[8] It was close to noon and a lull in the fighting occurred which was really only a brief respite for what was to come.

The second brigade of the Third Division under Colonel Roy Stone and the remainder of Wainwright's batteries, taking a different route from Biddle, had arrived at the Seminary earlier. Brigadier General John C. Robinson's Second Division also arrived there. Gabriel R. Paul's brigade of that division stopped momentarily and set to work constructing barricades at the bottom of the western side of the ridge just below the Seminary building.[9] Later in the afternoon that undertaking helped the hard-pressed Federals by creating a rallying point and protection against the final Confederate attack. The 151st Pennsylvania of Biddle's brigade was eventually left in reserve at the Seminary, occupying those breastworks after Paul's men marched north to join the rest of Robinson's division.[10]

Wainwright left two of his batteries, Stewart's and Stevens', south of the seminary buildings.[11] Later on, Stewart would be moved to the north of the Seminary buildings on both sides of an unfinished railroad cut that ran parallel to the Chambersburg Pike. Likewise, Stevens' battery would also be relocated north of the Seminary, south of the Chambersburg Pike. This shifting of Wainwright's batteries would continue all afternoon, depending on where the enemy threat existed. But this would also create conflict between Wainwright and infantry commanders who tried to usurp his authority and commandeer the guns for themselves.

Stone's brigade, known as the Bucktail Brigade from the deer tails the men wore on their caps in imitation of the 13th Pennsylvania Reserves, had come up from Seminary Ridge to connect with the Iron Brigade north of Herbst Woods. They took position between the woodlot and the Chambersburg Pike in a position just west of the McPherson Farm as Biddle's men arrived. The next phase of the battle was about to begin.

Wainwright really did not like the layout of the field from a tactical perspective. For one thing, the right flank was exposed to a high ridge to the north called Oak Hill, and approaches from that position had ravines that could conceal attacking units as they made their way toward that flank.[12] Wadsworth, though, was more interested in having the artillery support the infantry and had no compunctions in issuing direct orders to have batteries placed where he wanted them and without first conferring with Wainwright. Wainwright stopped Hall's battery responding to such a request, risking a potential confrontation with Wadsworth who had ordered that battery forward again.[13] In the absence of infantry support on the right, Wainwright

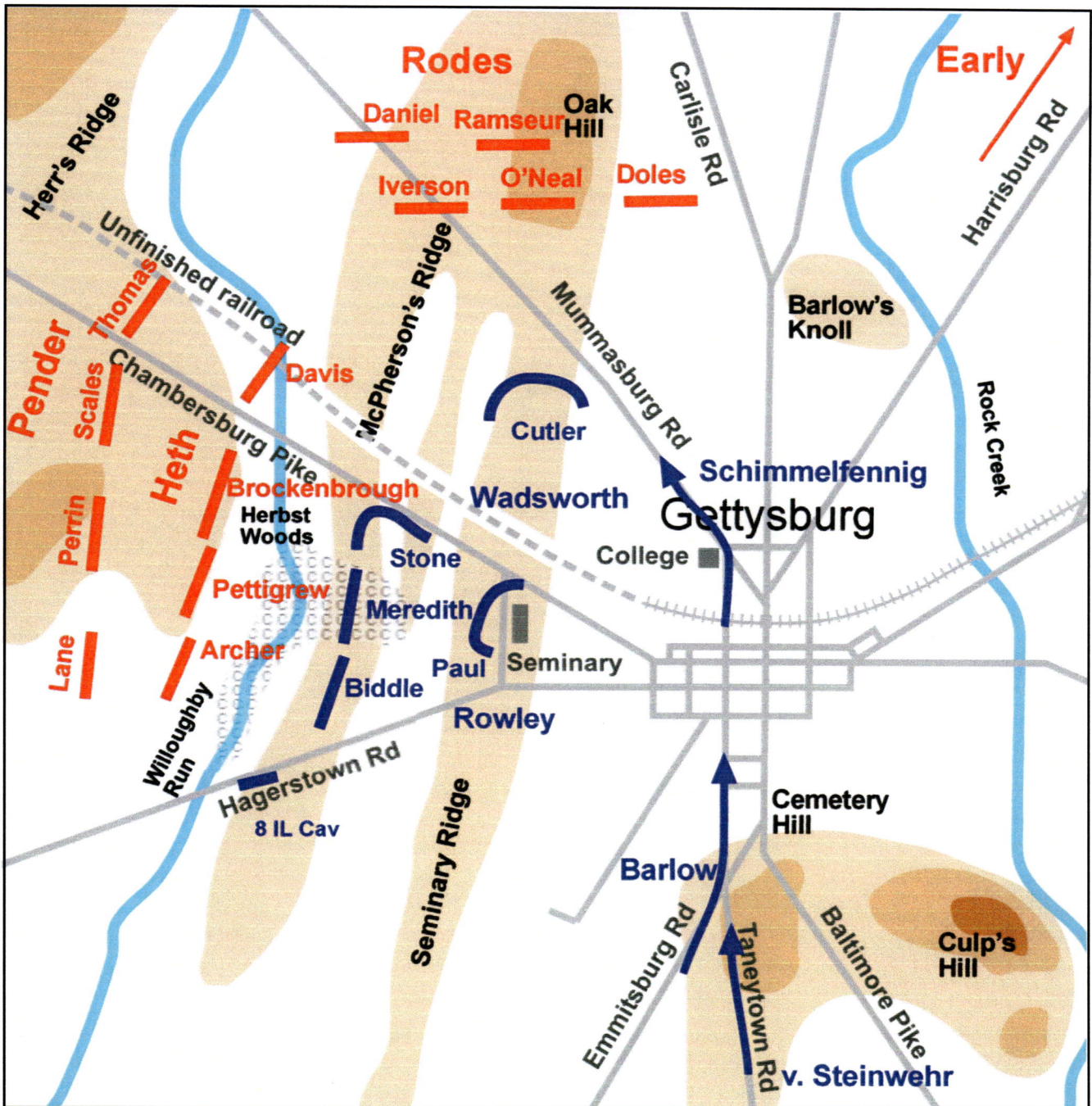

Cooper's initial position is with Biddle's brigade, south of Herbst Woods on the eastern side of McPherson Ridge. His four guns face west toward Herr Ridge. As Rodes approaches from the north near Oak Hill, Cooper is directed to shift his battery, now only three guns, to face north in the field between McPherson Ridge and the Seminary. Cooper engages in counterbattery fire with the artillery supporting Rodes.
(Map courtesy of Hal Jespersen's Wikipedia Civil War Maps)

felt that his guns were vulnerable to capture. Likewise, he stopped Gilbert Reynolds' battery which had been directed by Doubleday to support Calef's guns. After some discussion between himself and Doubleday, Wainwright let Reynolds go forward with the understanding that the battery would report to him and not Wadsworth.[14] It was split with one section under Lieutenant Wilbur positioned near the McPherson Farm buildings, and the other four guns located near the edge of Herbst's woodlot in support of Biddle.[15]

Meanwhile, Cooper's guns, already exposed on the crest further south, were subject to fire from Confederate sharpshooters who were positioned in a house and barn west of Biddle's line. A detachment from the 80th New York was sent there to clear them out.[16] Cooper's men then commenced counterbattery firing to the west against the Confederate guns on Herr Ridge.

Looking west in the front of Cooper's position near the Krauth House on Seminary Ridge. In the distance is McPherson Ridge which is marked by the white barn on the right and Herbst Woods on the left. Scales' brigade moved toward this position in the open field between these ridges on July 1 and was devastated by Wainwright's massed artillery fire.

After shooting off a few rounds, one of his guns sustained a broken axle from its recoil.[17] The remaining three kept firing, and after about 25 rounds, the Confederate fire from the west stopped.[18] But the break was short. Confederates were now approaching from the north in the area of Oak Hill. This was Major General Robert E. Rodes' division of Lieutenant General Richard S. Ewell's Second Corps. Lieutenant Colonel Thomas H. Carter set his artillery on the hill facing south to enfilade the Federals who faced west on McPherson Ridge. Everything that Wainwright had feared about the Federal position was soon to become a reality as William P. Carter's and Charles W. Fry's batteries announced Rodes' arrival by firing into that portion of the First Corps on the ridge.[19] The time was between 1:00 and 1:30 p.m., and now the Federals were subject to artillery crossfire from two directions, north as well as west.

To meet this threat, Cooper's, Reynolds', and Calef's guns shifted positions facing Oak Hill. Cooper's three guns moved from the crest of the eastern ridgeline of McPherson Ridge to the meadow in the rear of that position.[20] They fired over the Chambersburg Pike and railroad cut in counterbattery fire with Carter and Fry. It was a dangerous situation, and both Biddle's brigade on the eastern slope of the ridge and Stone's at the McPherson Farm had to change front to avoid the enfilading fire coming at them from Oak Hill. Biddle's men moved south toward the Fairfield Road and hunkered down behind a fence and roadbank facing north.[21] Brigadier General Lysander Cutler's brigade of Wadsworth's division located on the other side of the Chambersburg Pike moved back onto Seminary Ridge, providing a good alleyway for Cooper's and Reynolds' batteries to fire back at the Confederate artillery. But now Captain Reynolds was wounded and command passed to Lieutenant George Breck.[22]

At about 2:30 p.m., Cooper's gunners noticed that Confederate infantry was moving from Oak Hill southeast toward the area occupied by Robinson's division. This was Brigadier General Alfred Iverson's brigade of Rodes' force, which made an excellent target for them. Abandoning counterbattery fire for the moment, Cooper's men keyed on Iverson's brigade, pouring into it a "most galling and destructive front and flank fire of case shot."[23] Once Iverson's attack had been repulsed by Robinson's men, Brigadier General Junius Daniel's brigade made its try to attack Stone near the McPherson Farm building directly

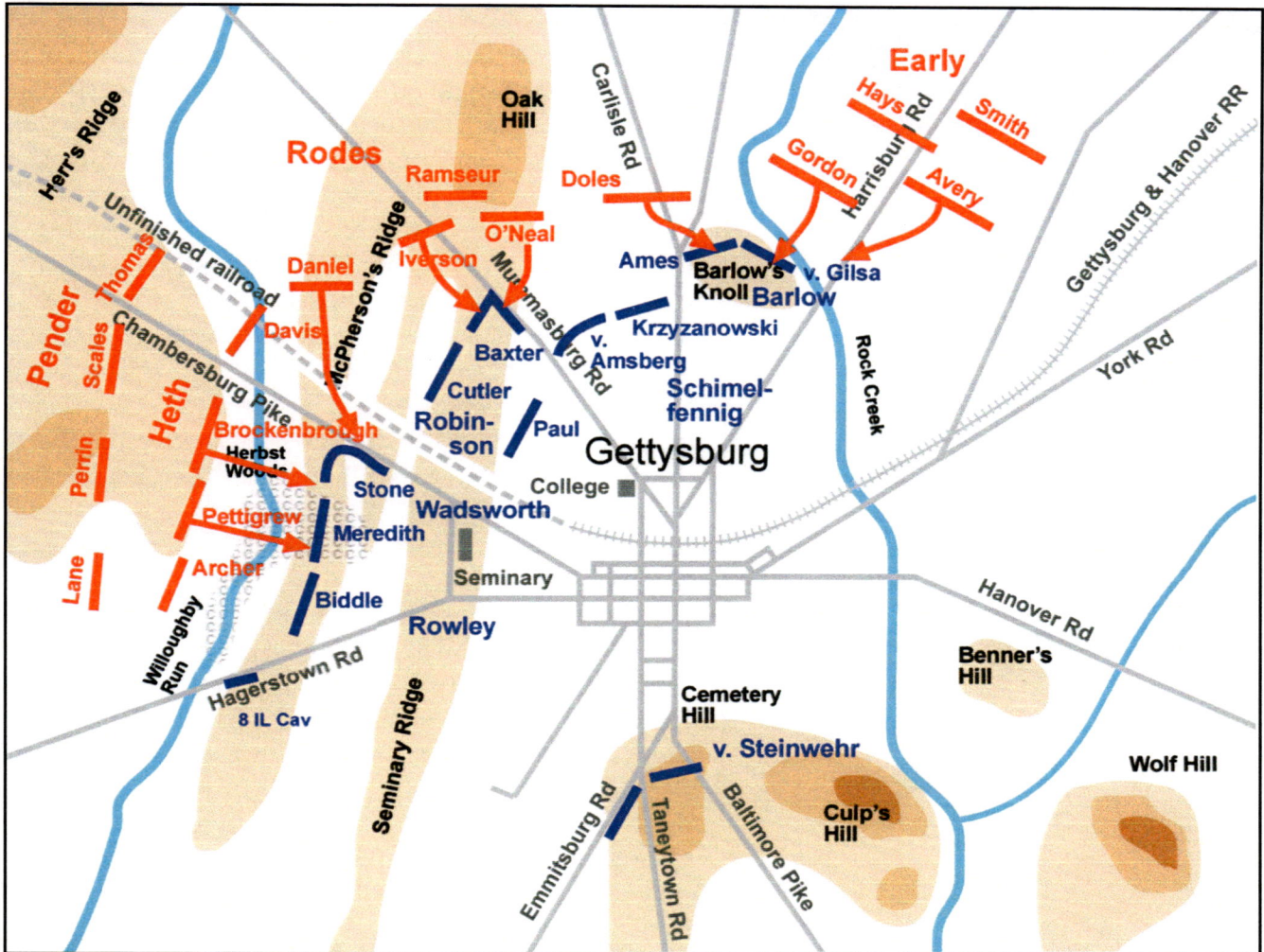

With the exception of Von Steinwehr's men left on Cemetery Hill by General Howard, the rest of the Eleventh Corps proceeds through town to take up a position north of it and perpendicular to the right flank of the First Corps. After getting there, the Eleventh Corps is attacked by Early's Division. Portions of Rodes' Division (O'Neal, Iverson, and Daniel) attack from the north against the First Corps but are repulsed. Cooper's battery, still facing north, also helps to stop Iverson and Daniel with artillery fire.
(Map courtesy of Hal Jespersen's Wikipedia Civil War Maps)

south of Oak Hill. Moving toward the Chambersburg Pike, Daniel's men were stopped just north of the railroad cut from the combination of infantry and cannon fire.[24] Cooper in his report indicated that his battery had only occupied this position for several minutes, but it is obvious from the amount of time these Confederate attacks took to develop as well as the counterbattery fire preceding it, the unit must have held this position for a longer period.[25]

Off to the north of Gettysburg, two divisions of Major General Oliver O. Howard's Federal Eleventh Corps were being deployed on a plain, having passed through the town from their approach on the Taneytown Road. They would be facing the attack of Major General Jubal A. Early's division of Ewell's Second Corps which was joining Rodes to bear down on the Federals from that direction. Howard retained one division on Cemetery Hill south of town which was a high and prominent elevation, a good defendable

James P. Alcorn who buried his brother on the field on July 1 and was captured.
(Courtesy of Kenneth C. Turner)

position should the Federals be required to withdraw. Some have credited Howard with realizing the tactical importance of Cemetery Hill, not only just from seeing it but also taking steps to ensure that there were men there to hold it.[26] This would prove to be a propitious decision.

The Eleventh Corps consisted of some regiments with a large percentage of non-native soldiers, mostly German, in its ranks who were also commanded by German-speaking officers in many instances.[27] Understandably, due to the foreign accents, communication problems would occur on occasions. According to Wainwright, one of Howard's German aides approached Doubleday, telling Doubleday that Major General Winfield S. Hancock had succeeded General Reynolds in the command of both corps and wanted Cemetery Hill to be held at all hazards. Wainwright related: "What with the aide's broken English and our being on this hill [Seminary Ridge] and not knowing that there was a *cemetery*, I thought it was the *Seminary* Hill we were to hold."[28]

Wainwright did not have much time to ascertain the correct interpretation of what he heard anyway. Confederate forces from the west under Lieutenant General A.P. Hill were about to attack McPherson Ridge again. Hill sent Brigadier General J.J. Pettigrew and Colonel J.M. Brockenbrough's brigades of Major General Henry Heth's division into the fight. The Iron Brigade and Stone's men, already tired and worn from fighting earlier, could not withstand the pressure from these two fresh Confederate brigades despite their best efforts. Biddle, too, could not contain Pettigrew's attack, even with the help of the 151st Pennsylvania which was recalled from the Seminary to bolster his line.[29]

Wainwright proceeded to mass his batteries at the Seminary to hold that position based on what he overheard Howard's aide tell Doubleday. Among them was Cooper's which was relocated from the meadow back toward the Seminary near the Krauth House. Cooper's guns faced west far behind the breastworks that were constructed earlier in the day. It was now about 3:00 p.m.[30] Captain T.A. Brander's Virginia Battery located on a hill north of the railroad cut began shelling Cooper's position. At the same time, the Confederate infantry made another try to drive off Stone's brigade from north of the railroad cut. Notwithstanding a cross-fire from Fry's battery on Oak Hill, Cooper was able to engage in effective counter-battery fire with Brander's guns as well as assist Stone's men.[31] He also was able to shell Pettigrew's troops who were moving against the rest of the Federal line.[32]

But the pressure was just too great for the infantry on McPherson Ridge. They were being outflanked. The Eleventh Corps was also having its problems north of town trying to contain Early's attack. Robinson's men on the extreme right of the First Corps line could see the implications of being attacked in their rear as well as from the front if the Eleventh Corps vacated its position. Gradually, the Federals were being forced to fall back. Even more foreboding now was the fact that yet another fresh Confederate force consisting of Colonel Abner Perrin's and Brigadier General A. M. Scales' brigades passed over Pettigrew's and Brockenbrough's men, heading straight for the Seminary from McPherson Ridge.[33]

Doubleday placed Stevens' guns, previously south of the Seminary, to Cooper's right. Almost immediately, Stevens began to fire over the heads of the retreating Federals.[34] With the addition of Wilbur's section of Reynolds' battery to the right of Stevens, the cannons there were squeezed so tight that only five yards separated each gun.[35] Across the Chambersburg Pike, Stewart's battery had six guns, straddling both sides of the railroad cut, the closest to the Seminary being the three guns of Lieutenant Davison's section.[36]

For Cooper's men, it must have looked like Fredericksburg all over again with Perrin and Scales coming right at them. Remnants of Biddle's, Stone's, and Meredith's brigades established a line on the western slope of Seminary Ridge around the buildings, some settling down behind the barricades there and preparing themselves to hold off this new onslaught. Wainwright's artillery was also ready.

Perrin and Scales moved east down the meadow across where Cooper's battery had been positioned earlier when it engaged in counterbattery fire with Carter's guns on Oak Hill. It was close to 4:00 p.m. The sweaty and tired Federals still had fight left in them as they waited. Scales' brigade was the closest to the pike and was headed for Wainwright's artillery where Stone's men and the Iron Brigade stood. Further to the south, Perrin's brigade was on a direct line toward the Seminary itself where Biddle's men were located.

Once Scales' men approached within 100 yards of the Federal position, Wainwright's artillery raked their line.[37] Firing case shot, shell, and canister, all fourteen guns of Cooper's and Stevens' batteries along with Wilbur's and Davison's sections of their respective batteries, threw Scales' men into confusion and broke them up.[38] The Federal line of battle was characterized as a "continuous blaze of fire" with the space between McPherson and Seminary Ridges completely filled with smoke and making it nearly impossible to tell friend from foe.[39] Colonel William Robinson of the 7th Wisconsin Infantry was positioned in front of the guns with his men and wrote that the Confederate ranks

Professor Krauth's home on Seminary Ridge where James P. Alcorn's brother died, the house showing a post-battle addition on the right that did not exist then.

went down "like grass before the scythe from the united fire of our regiments and the battery. There were very few, if any, of that brigade [that] escaped death or wounds."[40] Not only was Scales himself hit, but every field officer, save one, of his five regiments was either killed or wounded as well.[41]

Then moving aside some infantry at the breastworks, Cooper trained his guns slightly left on Perrin's men. The musketry of the infantry and the artillery's canister fire nearly annihilated Perrin's left flank, that portion being swept away entirely from the front of Cooper's guns with only a single rebel color bearer reaching the rail barricade in front of the battery.[42] When the fire first came, Perrin's left-most regiment, the 14th South Carolina, felt the effect of the artillery the most. It faltered for a moment before proceeding forward without halting and firing in return. As one officer said: "To stop was destruction. To retreat was disaster. To go forward was 'orders.'"[43] The Federal infantry now added to destructive power of the artillery, rising up and pouring in a volley at Perrin's men. Dark clouds of smoke obscured vision, but to Perrin it looked as though the entire 14th was destroyed.[44]

Perrin, seeing that his men were being torn up by the combined Federal infantry and artillery fire, directed the 1st South Carolina to proceed against a weak part of the Federal line to its right and then swing left against the Federals positioned at the breastworks.[45] After coming around, the 1st South Carolina was then in position to enfilade the Federals behind their works. The whole Federal line was crumbling at the Seminary now;[46] but Wainwright, still thinking that he was to defend Seminary Ridge to the last, refused to have his batteries leave, notwithstanding Wadsworth's directive to Stevens to pull out his guns.[47] When the Eleventh Corps totally disintegrated north of town, it was not long before Robinson's and Wadsworth's divisions came filing over the railroad cut. Witnessing this, Wainwright changed his mind and ordered the batteries out.[48]

THE LAST STAND

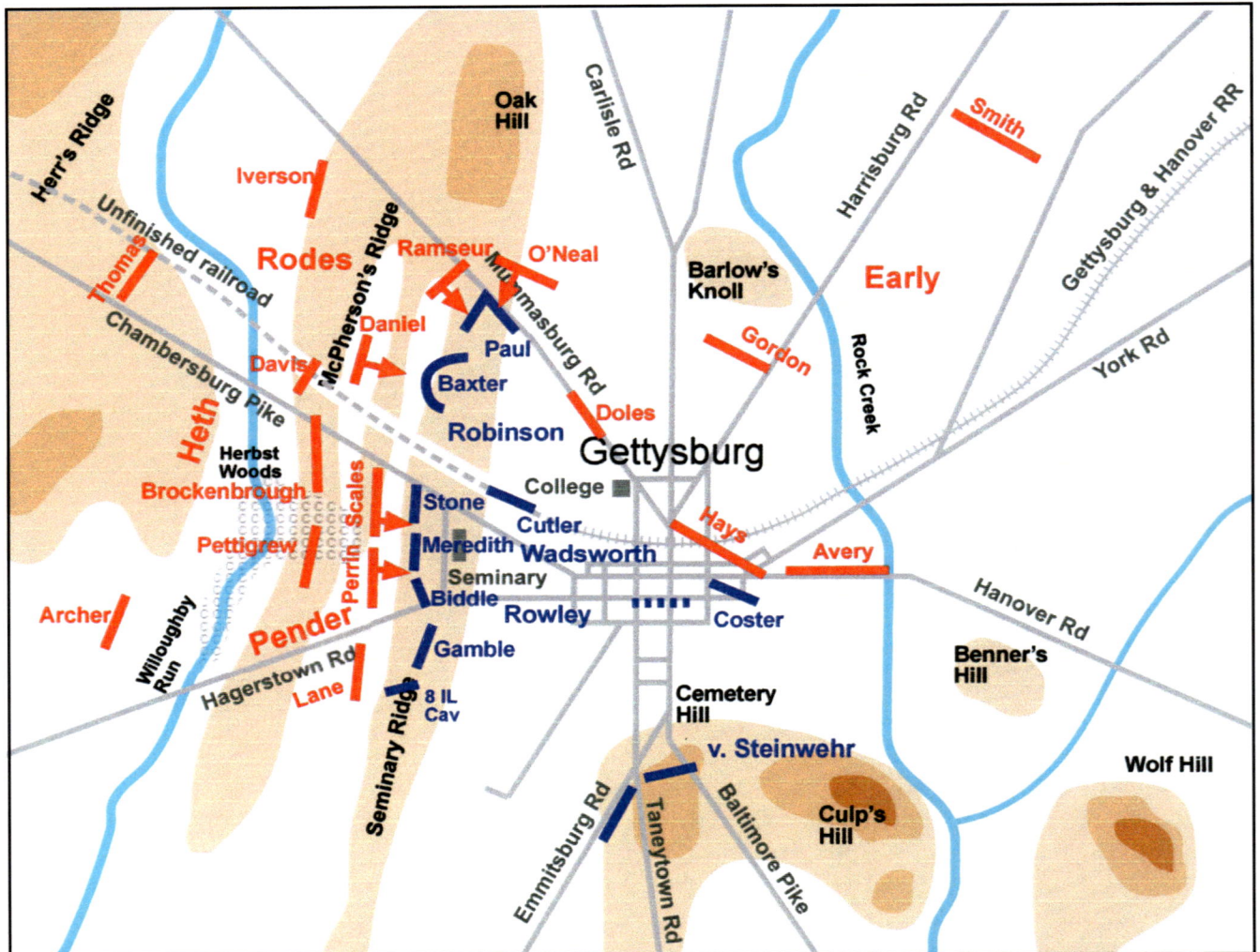

The Eleventh Corps can no longer stand the pressure from Early's attack and is being forced back through the town to Cemetery Hill. Rodes renews his attack on the First Corps from the north while Confederate attacks from the west force Stone's, Meredith's, and Biddle's brigades back to the barricade in front of the Seminary. Wainwright has massed his batteries in the vicinity of the Seminary, awaiting the final onslaught by Scales' and Perrin's brigades which have passed over Pettigrew's men and press on, intent on forcing the Federals from Seminary Ridge. The defensive line at the Seminary will crumble despite the stand made by the Federals there. Meanwhile the right flank of the First Corps' line has given way and is streaming back toward the town. Cooper's battery is directed to fall back with the other batteries. It establishes itself on the eastern portion of Cemetery Hill facing Benner's Hill with the Baltimore Pike in its rear. The rest of the Federal army coalesces in the area as the Confederates pursue them through the town, capturing many prisoners. (Map courtesy of Hal Jespersen's Wikipedia Civil War Maps)

As Cooper limbered up and wheeled to the right to get on the Chambersburg Pike, Stevens was also leaving. Cooper shouted out to Lieutenant Edward N. Whittier of Steven's battery, "Hell's to pay, Ned!"[49] This was certainly no exaggeration, given the situation at the time. Both batteries became intermingled in their withdrawal down the Chambersburg Pike to the succor of Cemetery Hill where General Howard had set up a rallying position earlier in the day. The roads were filled with retreating Federal infantry units and stragglers who encumbered the quick withdrawal of the artillery. As they left, some of the batteries sustained damage to their guns and caissons, and some had to be abandoned.[50] When the Confederates poured over the southern part of the Seminary building, they let loose on Federal infantry on the Chambersburg Pike. Diving for cover in the security of the railroad bed on the other side, the infantry actually cleared the roadway for Wainwright's batteries to proceed. He gave the command to "Trot" and then "Gallop" and off they went three abreast.[51]

Two brothers of Cooper's battery never made it back, though. Before proceeding to limber up the guns, Sergeant James P. Alcorn gave the command "left about" to get the left section ready.[52] The off horse in the lead fell dead and threw the head horse and driver, pinning down the man for a time until he could be extricated by his comrades. But James' brother, Alexander, was not as lucky. When Cooper had given the command to limber up, Confederate infantry fire found its mark and Alexander was wounded. Once the sections of the battery were formed and underway, James returned to the Seminary, looking for Alexander, and was told that some wounded artillerymen were being carried to a little brick house there. James was now between two lines firing at each other, the Federals withdrawing and the Confederates pursuing. Riding a horse, he jumped the garden fence in the front of the building and went inside. There he found Privates Jesse Temple and Peter G. Hoagland of the battery bringing Alexander through the door.[53]

At the time, the house was being riddled with bullets from both sides. Removing Alexander's clothing, James found that his brother had been wounded at the lower end of the spine with the bullet passing out at the thigh, crushing the pelvis bone and severing the main artery of his leg. While attempting to stop the bleeding, James told Temple and Hoagland to get out, using the building as cover until they reached the railroad cut for protection. Both made it back and re-joined the battery.[54]

James stayed with his brother as the Confederates swept over Seminary Ridge. As a result, he, too, was captured. That evening Alexander died, and James had the sad task of burying him. But before he could finish, his captors ordered him to move out with other prisoners back to Cashtown.[55]

The results of the action on the first day were particularly hard on the artillery batteries which were moved from place to place as needed and were subject to conflicting orders from Wadsworth, Doubleday, and Wainwright at various times.[56] Cooper's Battery B was no exception to those being shunted about the field. It had occupied three different positions and fired over 400 rounds, most of which came from only three guns. Later that evening the damaged gun was repaired. Beside the loss of Alexander Alcorn and the capture of his brother, four other men were wounded.[57] When he arrived at Cemetery Hill, Cooper was directed by General Doubleday to establish and strengthen the lines. He also conferred directly with General Hancock and Brigadier General Adelbert Ames.[58]

The battle that day was over for Cooper's men, but they had little rest. By next morning, they had finished the construction of four lunettes on East Cemetery Hill to shield their guns which faced east.[59] Since the Confederates did not exploit their success by trying to force the Federals off Cemetery Hill after driving them through the town, Cooper's men would have to wait to see what would happen next. July 2 would prove to be yet another difficult test for the Army of the Potomac as General Robert E. Lee conceived a plan to attack them again rather than disengage and fight elsewhere.

GETTYSBURG—DAY TWO

General Hancock was a source of inspiration to the beleaguered remnants of the First and Eleventh Corps as they made their way through town to Cemetery Hill late on July 1. He projected self-assurance and confidence, something which the soldiers sorely needed at that juncture. One story is that Lieutenant Whittier of Stevens' battery approached Hancock wanting to know where he would like the battery placed. Pointing to the knoll on the slope of Culp's Hill which was adjacent to East Cemetery Hill, Hancock said: "Do you see that hill, young man? Put your battery there and stay there." [60] Hancock was sent by Meade to ascertain the condition of the army and to take command in his absence. Even though General Howard was senior in rank on the field, Hancock assumed overall authority for the management of army at that point based on Meade's specific directive.

Meade arrived as the tired men slept on their arms that night. The rest of the Army of the Potomac was moving up, and it seemed inevitable that Gettysburg would be the place where the two antagonists would continue the fighting. [61] For his part, Wainwright had assumed command of the batteries on Cemetery Hill at General Howard's suggestion when Cooper's and Stevens' guns first arrived there. [62] Captain Michael Wiedrich's 1st New York Battery I of four guns was already on the northern part of East Cemetery Hill, being part of the Eleventh Corps artillery brigade. Wainwright positioned Cooper's battery to Wiedrich's right on the other side of a stone wall separating them. Next to Cooper's right was a gun from Stewart's battery and then Reynolds' five guns under the command of Breck, being recessed slightly behind Cooper. Stewart's other smoothbores were stationed directly behind Cooper near the cemetery gatehouse to fire down the Baltimore Pike if the enemy tried to come up from the town. As mentioned earlier, once Stevens' battery arrived, it was directed to the northern slope of Culp's Hill above the ravine separating it from East Cemetery Hill. A total of twenty guns aimed northeast to stop any Confederate threat from that direction. [63]

Major Thomas W. Osborn formed the rest of his Eleventh Corps' batteries on the other side of the Baltimore Pike, behind the gatehouse among the gravestones facing north toward the town. It must have created some humor for the artillerymen when they saw a sign near the entrance of the cemetery stating that all persons found using firearms in those grounds would be legally prosecuted. [64] During the morning at about 9:30 a.m., Cooper's gunners fired on some moving columns of enemy infantry and cavalry about a mile away, but they only discharged about 25 rounds. Confederate cannons on

CEMETERY HILL

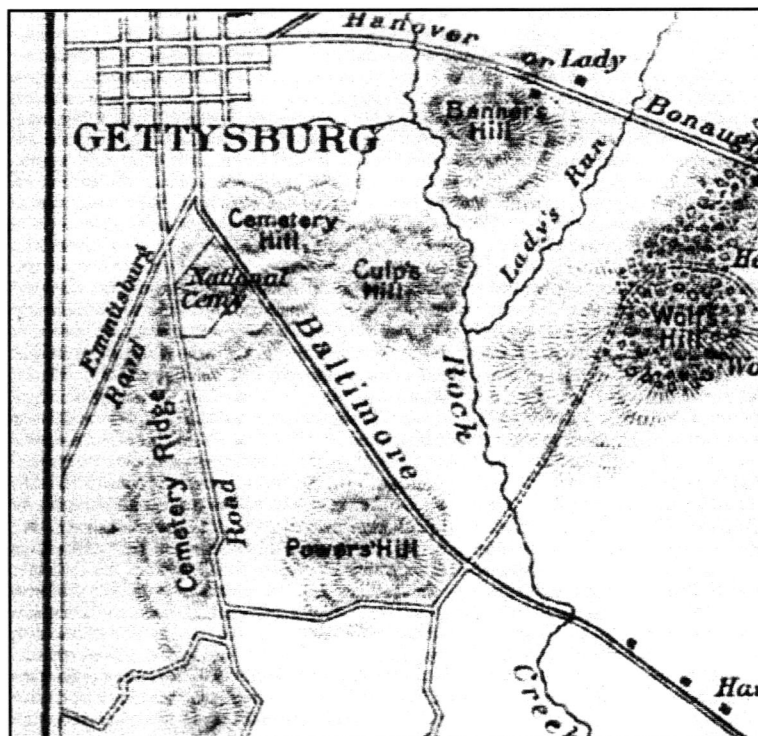

View of East Cemetery Hill and Benner's Hill where the artillery duel took place between Wainwright's and Osborn's batteries and those of Latimer on the afternoon of July 2. (Portion of map taken from Field of Cavalry Operations, East of Gettysburg, July 2nd and 3rd, Library of Congress Collection)

Seminary Ridge also fired at Cemetery Hill, the rebel gunners apparently seeking to establish the range.[65]

The rest of the Federal army had come up during the night and early morning. The Sixth Corps was still en route and had to make a forced march to get to the field later in the day. As both armies formed their lines, Lee's army occupied the town and encircled the area east of Cemetery Hill. The Confederates eventually extended their position along the left flank of the Federals with two divisions of Lieutenant General James Longstreet's corps moving south along Seminary Ridge to prepare for an assault that would hopefully roll up that flank. Meade's army, along Cemetery Ridge, occupied a position roughly mirroring the Confederate line, having the inside track of what appeared to be two concentric lines facing each other. The Federal position was stronger for defense because its interior line was shorter, allowing units to be transferred to affected sectors much easier and more quickly. While Cemetery Hill and Culp's Hill were high points on the Federal right flank and already manned with troops, the higher points along the left flank further south, namely Little and Big Round Tops, were yet unoccupied with an appreciable force. That would change later in the day as Longstreet began his attack, forcing Meade to transfer troops there.

Nothing significant occurred for the battery until about 4:00 p.m. when Con-

Three-inch Ordinance Rifle Gun, being the type used by Cooper's Battery at Gettysburg.
(Photo taken at Gettysburg National Military Park)

Parrott Rifled Gun, being the type used by Cooper's Battery earlier in the war.
(Photo taken at Gettysburg National Military Park)

federate artillery fire from Benner's Hill and other nearby areas focused on the Federal artillery on East Cemetery Hill. These were mainly the 14 guns of Major Joseph W. Latimer's artillery battalion on Benner's Hill, a plateau elevation approximately 1500 yards away from East Cemetery Hill to the east beyond Rock Creek and along the Hanover Road. The crest of Benner's Hill was relatively open, only having some wheat and knee-high corn growing there which was insufficient to conceal the guns. While the artillery on Benner's Hill could fire upon Cemetery Hill, only one battery on the left could do so against Culp's Hill. Conversely, Federal batteries on Culp's Hill and the knoll occupied by Stevens as well as batteries on East Cemetery Hill could easily concentrate all their fire upon Benner's Hill.[66]

Facing Benner's Hill were the long-range and accurate three-inch ordnance rifles of Wiedrich, Cooper, and Breck. Off to the right on the slope of Culp's Hill were Stevens' six smoothbore 12-pound Napoleons.[67] The Napoleons which had slightly less range and accuracy shot a spherical projectile while the rifled pieces fired conical ones. But at close range the Napoleons were more effective because they could discharge larger loads of canister due to the larger diameter of the bore. The effect of canister from a smoothbore gun was also more lethal because once the container ruptured inside the barrel, the iron balls inside could disperse in a wider pattern. That is why Stewart's and Stevens' guns were so effective against Scales and Perrin at the Seminary on July 1. But now, the threat from Benner's Hill called for accurate long-range counterbattery fire that made the rifled pieces more effective.[68] Wainwright potentially had about ten rifled guns of Osborn at his disposal located across the Baltimore Pike facing Benner's Hill that could add to his firepower.[69]

Latimer had Graham's Rockinbridge (Virginia) Battery of four 20-pound Parrotts at his disposal to augment his own batteries. Left of Graham's unit was Brown's Chesapeake (Maryland) Battery of four 10-pound Parrott guns. Next was Carpenter's Allegheny (Virginia) Battery of two three-inch rifles and two

Breech end of Parrott Rifled Gun showing wrought iron reinforcing band. (Photo taken at Gettysburg National Military Park)

light 12-pounders, followed by Dement's First Maryland of four light 12-pounders. Finally, Raine's Lee (Virginia) Battery, consisting of a 10-pound Parrott and a three-inch rifle piece, completed the complement of guns on the hill. But Latimer also had Raines' two 20-pounder Parrotts off to the right beyond the Hanover Road. They were bigger and could fire larger projectiles further.[70] The Confederates had guns on Seminary Ridge to the west that were trained on Cemetery Hill, too.[71]

Confederate Major General Edward Johnson had ordered Latimer onto Benner's Hill and instructed him to open fire with all his guns. Latimer did so once he got into position. The Federal guns on East Cemetery Hill and those of Osborn behind them replied with vigor. John Hatton of Dement's battery maintained that the firing produced "a continuous vibration like a severe storm raging in the elements." He felt that "Benner's Hill was simply a Hell infernal." Men and horses became casualties. The Confederate batteries on Seminary Ridge added to what was hitting the Federal gunners from Benner's Hill. One writer noted that the storm of shot and shell had broken the slabs in the cemetery, shattered iron fences, and disemboweled horses. He said: "The air was filled with wild, hideous noises, the low buzz of round shot, the whizzing of elongated

12-Pound Smoothbore Napoleon Cannon of the type used by Stewart's and Stevens' Batteries most effectively on July 1. (Photo taken at Gettysburg National Military Park)

balls and the stunning explosion of shells overhead and all around."[72]

The fire near Cooper's position was particularly severe. One of his first shots blew up a Confederate caisson. This prompted Stewart's gunners to raise a cheer. Just then a Confederate shell came down on Stewart's caisson, sending the chests skyward and causing horses to run off, some with the hair on their manes and tails burned. A while later, another one blew up Stewart's limber.[73] A shell struck and exploded at Cooper's No. 3 gun, killing or wounding every man servicing that piece. But before the wounded were cleared out, the gun was back in operation with a new crew.[74] Another shell struck and broke the axle of the No. 2 gun, but the firing from that cannon continued unabated until near the close of the action when the entire carriage broke down.[75] Years later, James A. Gardner of the battery described the scene on East Cemetery Hill:

Limber that was used to pull artillery and caissons. (Photo taken at Gettysburg National Military Park)

....*The shots of the enemy came thick and fast, bursting, crushing and ploughing, a mighty storm of iron hail, a most determined and terrible effort of the enemy to cripple and destroy the guns on the hill. Situated as we were in the center of the artillery line, our battery received the full force of the enemy's front, oblique and flank fire. Against the batteries on Seminary Ridge we were powerless; but*

Limber to which is attached a caisson that contained extra ammunition and a spare pole and wheel. (Photo taken at Gettysburg National Military Park)

17

upon the batteries of Latimer on Benner's Hill, and upon Graham and Raine to our left, an accurate and most telling fire was opened from the batteries on this hill [Cemetery Hill] and continued for about two hours. [76]

Wainwright sat with General Adelbert Ames on the stone wall separating Weidrich's and Cooper's batteries simply surveying the action. He saw a shot go through two or three yards of Federal infantrymen lying behind it in which at least a dozen or so were killed or wounded. So close was the impact that it covered him with dust. On another occasion when standing close to Wiedrich's guns, a shell plowed into the ground near his feet. Wainwright calmly contemplated whether it would explode from the entrance hole or straight up. He was fortunate—it went out the hole.[77]

Wainwright thought that Cooper's and Reynolds' (Breck's) batteries fired "beautifully." Ames concurred. The contrast with Wiedrich's gunners was apparent. Wainwright felt that Wiedrich's men were ignorant of ranges, and he had to set the sight on each piece and show the gunners the length of fuse to use.[78] He was particularly impressed with Cooper's battery after the incident involving gun No. 3:

View of Battery B's position looking toward the stone wall separating it from Wiedrich's guns on East Cemetery Hill.

Position of Battery B on East Cemetery Hill looking toward Benner's Hill.

Joseph Reed, wounded on July 2. (Courtesy of Kenneth C. Turner)

Here I had a specimen of the stuff this battery is composed of, and forgave Cooper and his men their utter unmilitariness and loose ideas of discipline in camp. So soon as the shell burst I jumped from the wall, and told Cooper to put on another detachment, that General Ames would let some of his men carry off the wounded; not a murmur was uttered, but five other men at once took place over their dead and wounded comrades, and fired before they could be removed. I was very proud of it.[79]

He noted that one of those cannoneers was blown to pieces, losing his right hand, his left arm at the shoulder, and his ribs so broken that he could see through him. Cooper asked Wainwright for permission to have the brother of the mortally wounded man be with him while he lived. According to Wainwright, even though the brother was only the bugler of the battery and was really not needed to service the guns, he remained with them and would not leave unless granted permission to do so. Nor would Cooper grant such permission without first asking Wainwright. At any other time when the battery was in camp, the men would go off all day without permission and Cooper would overlook it.[80] But in battle the situation was different.

Wainwright was impressed with the accuracy of Confederate fire and was surprised that more damage was not done, particularly among the horses crowded together with the limbers.[81] But gradually, the superior firepower and position of the Federal batteries began to take its toll on the more exposed Confederate ones on Benner's Hill.[82] Stevens' battery and some guns brought up by Brigadier General John W. Geary of the Twelfth Corps atop Culp's Hill were effective to help those on East Cemetery Hill. Captain Brown of the Chesapeake Artillery was mortally wounded early on. Other Confederate cannoneers were blown to pieces. When one gunner wondered why his gun was not being supplied with ammunition, he approached the limber and inquired of the chief of the piece where the rest of the crew was located. He was shown one man cut in half and two others without heads. As the two conversed, another shell exploded in the ground disemboweling one of the limber drivers and killing two horses.[83]

The Chesapeake Artillery could only use two guns, the others being damaged, and then those had to be brought off by hand.[84] When Latimer recognized that he could not continue, he requested permission to abandon Benner's Hill. General Johnson granted his request in part, requiring that Latimer leave four pieces there to support an infantry advance that would take place against Culp's Hill. When those four guns opened up again, they drew a horrendous fire in return. During the exchange, Latimer was mortally wounded and he would die the following month, not yet 21 years of age.[85] So great was the Federal cannonade that afterward there were 28 dead horses found on the hill.[86] Lieutenant Breck indicated that he found three disabled cannons abandoned there.[87]

According to Wainwright's report, Cooper's battery also suffered considerably.[88] At about 7:00 p.m., it was relieved by Captain R. Bruce Ricketts' battery of the Artillery Reserve

John M. Fullerton who was a sergeant in the battery at Gettysburg.
(Courtesy of Kenneth C. Turner)
He survived the war without injury even though a horse he was riding in one battle was decapitated and another one was killed by a cannon ball that struck the saddle flap. His luck ended in 1912 when, ironically, a streetcar ran into his buggy, this time killing both the horse and him along with a companion. (From: History of the Family of James Fullerton and Margaret Sharp, p. 100— supplied by Nancy Gardner)

which occupied Cooper's lunettes. One of Rickett's gunners found a severed hand belonging to one of Cooper's men and buried it on the lunette.[89]

While engaged that day, Cooper's battery fired 500 rounds, about 475 being consumed from his duel with Latimer.[90] More significant was the loss of additional men. Peter G. Hoagland, who helped carry James Alcorn's wounded brother to one of the Seminary buildings the day before, was now mortally wounded himself and would die at the artillery brigade hospital. Also mortally wounded was James H. McCleary.[91] Among the other injured or wounded artillerymen was Jesse Temple who accompanied Hoagland in carrying James' brother back. He sustained severe wounds in both arms and thigh.[92] The battery lost one horse killed and two others which were totally disabled and abandoned.[93]

One gun of the battery sustained some damage toward the end of the engagement, and all the ammunition was depleted, the men having had to borrow some from an adjoining battery in order to continue firing. Wainwright directed Cooper to the Artillery Reserve to refit and replenish the ammunition chests. As the battery proceeded down the Baltimore Pike and turned to the right by a barn to get to Brigadier General Robert O. Tyler's Artillery Reserve camp, the men were understandably exhausted and saddened by the loss of their comrades. Some probably felt that they would never again experience the type of artillery bombardment they were subjected to that afternoon. The battery stayed at camp until the following day.[94] But the men would be called out again in yet another artillery duel that far surpassed any of their expectations.

GETTYSBURG—DAY THREE

About the same time as the artillery duel began between Latimer and Federal guns on East Cemetery Hill in the late afternoon of July 2, the Confederates were getting prepared to attack the Federal left flank further south. Severe fighting dissipated the strength of both armies in that sector as General Lee unsuccessfully tried to roll up the Federals there, his men having to contend with four Federal infantry corps that were thrown into the vortex of battle. The coordinated en echelon attack envisioned by Lee failed as separate firefights occurred in such areas as Devil's Den, Little Round Top, the Wheatfield, Peach Orchard, and Plum Run. Latimer's bombardment was a prelude to General Johnson's infantry assault of Culp's Hill that evening which was part of Lee's plan to try to coordinate an attack on the right flank as well. Confederates also attacked East Cemetery Hill. Fortunately, Cooper's battery missed that engagement as Rickett's gunners took the brunt of the Confederate assault, forcing them to engage in hand to hand fighting along the line of guns before Federal infantry drove off the attackers.[95] By now, Meade's position looked impregnable with his line resembling a fishhook stretching from Culp's Hill on the right, bending around Cemetery Hill, and going south to Little Round Top. With both flanks securely resting on elevations, the Army of the Potomac waited for Lee's next move.

Fighting again erupted in the early morning of July 3 at Culp's Hill, and it became obvious to Cooper's men that Lee was not about to quit yet. It was now 11:00 a.m. and Cooper was ready for action, having repaired one of his guns damaged in the duel with Latimer and filling up his caissons with fresh ammunition.

The Confederate commander now intended to attack the Federal center on Cemetery Ridge with his only remaining fresh division under the command of Major General George E. Pickett of Longstreet's First Corps as well as the two tested divisions of A.P. Hill's Corps, namely Major General Harry Heth's (now commanded by Pettigrew) and Major General William D. Pender's (now under the command of Major General Isaac R. Trimble). These two divisions had engaged the Federal First Corps on July 1 and included the remnants of Scales' and Perrin's brigades which suffered so much from Wainwright's artillery

View looking south along South Hancock Avenue from the Pennsylvania Memorial. McGilvery's batteries were positioned along this front facing west on July 3 during the cannonade and subsequent Confederate infantry assault against Cemetery Ridge. In the foreground is the monument to the 1st Minnesota Infantry which sustained huge losses fighting in the Plum Run area on July 2. The George Weikert farm is in the distance. The National Park Service's marker for Cooper's battery is located next to the 1st Minnesota monument on the other side of the single cannon. Actually, the battery was located further south on this line.

on that day. Pickett and the others would be supported on the right by Brigadier General Cadmus M. Wilcox's and Colonel David Lang's brigades of Major General R.H. Anderson's division (A.P. Hill's Corps). The entire assault of approximately 14,000 men was to proceed east across the field from Seminary Ridge nearly a mile away from the Federals.[96] Longstreet, whose responsibility was to coordinate the attack, was not confident of success and was, therefore, reluctant to make it. The Confederates would be moving across relatively open fields with some ravines to shield them momentarily, but their assault would certainly not be concealed. As they proceeded toward their target they would be subjected to artillery fire from the guns on Cemetery Ridge and Little Round Top. Should Pickett's, Pettigrew's, and Trimble's men be able to cross the Emmitsburg Road between the lines, they would also face murderous fire from the packed Federal infantry awaiting them. Further south, once Wilcox's and Lang's men reached the Plum Run swale, Federal guns would be able to train on them most effectively.

Preparatory to the advance, General Lee, in classic fashion, planned to have a thorough artillery bombardment of the entire Federal position from Cemetery Hill south along the ridge. The task of massing the batteries, which numbered a total of 135 guns, [97] was assigned to a young artillery officer named Colonel Edward Porter Alexander. This was perhaps the largest concentration of Confederate artillery on any battlefield in the war.[98] Colonel Alexander was also entrusted by Longstreet to advise Pickett when to begin the attack based on Alexander's own assessment of when reduction of any Federal counterbattery fire made it appropriate. This was a huge responsibility to place on the young subordinate to say the least.

Facing Alexander's guns were clusters of Federal artillery under the overall control of Brigadier General Henry J. Hunt, Chief of Artillery. At Little Round Top, the elevation on the left flank of the Army of the Potomac, were some long-range Parrott guns of Lieutenant Benjamin Rittenhouse. North of Little

Round Top along Cemetery Ridge were over 30 guns under the command of Lieutenant Colonel Freeman McGilvery who ordered that some small earthworks be constructed to protect them. Rising ground to the west protected his batteries from Confederate artillery fire but an open corridor to the northwest allowed him to use enfilade fire on any attackers coming across the field.[99]

Another pocket of Hunt's artillery was located further north along a stone wall running north and south that angled east a short distance before resuming north to an area below Cemetery Hill called Ziegler's Grove. Finally, there were Osborn's guns atop Cemetery Hill that could face southwest to add to the mix. The Federals had about 126 total pieces in position that would play a part in the coming action.[100]

At 1:00 p.m. Colonel Alexander unleashed his cannons on the Federal line. From his vantage point, Osborn described the scene:

It is now conceded that never in any battle in the world was the fire of light artillery so heavy as that at Gettysburg. Every gun on the line in both armies was doing its best. The fire of both armies was excellent. Looking down our own line or along the enemy's line, there was not half a minute that one could not see the smoke from an exploded ammunition chest. A shell or solid shot striking a chest exploded it, and the white smoke from the powder shot up in a solid cloud which could be seen from every part of the army. These explosions were an indication of the accuracy of the fire and the damage being done by the fire of the opposing armies. More shot and shell killed men and horses than hit the small ammunition chests.[101]

Osborn also described the sound as "deafening," although as an artilleryman it did not affect him as much as it did the infantry.[102]

Confederate artillery fire seemed more concentrated in the area north of McGilvery's line where those batteries sustained large casualties and guns were virtually wrecked. Even so, many of the projectiles overshot their mark which perhaps limited the destruction that could have occurred. By comparison, McGilvery's line, protected by the higher ground to its west, was largely ignored by Confederate artillery. After awhile, McGilvery ignored them as well. He and General Hunt realized that the artillery fire from the enemy was a prelude to an infantry attack, and there was no reason to consume precious ammunition that could be more effectively used to stop it.

For the infantry, counterbattery fire, even if ineffective, served to bolster the morale of the soldier who had to withstand enemy shelling in such situations. General Hancock rode up and down his line on Cemetery Ridge during the cannonade, trying by his self-confident presence to raise the spirits of his infantrymen. Federal artillery firing back at the enemy would certainly help his efforts. There was a confrontation between Hancock and McGilvery over this issue, but the latter refused to back down, particularly since he was not under Hancock's control to begin with. Here again was another instance in which an infantry officer tried to interfere with the artillery.[103]

Hunt ordered up more artillery from the Reserve, one of these being Cooper's battery. James A. Gardner recalled the scene years later:

In coming to this position, we passed through a terrible fire at its height, cutting and slashing, and crashing against the rocks; the troops were hugging the ground, and sheltering behind earth, stone and everything and anything which would seem to give protection.[104]

Cooper was directed to McGilvery's line to relieve another battery there, and as Battery B unlimbered and got into position, it immediately turned its attention on some Confederate guns to its front. Completely neutralizing them after a few shots, Cooper was ordered to cease fire.[105]

As the cannonade seemed to abate itself, the men realized what would take place next. Pickett's, Pettigrew's, and Trimble's divisions moved out toward Cemetery Ridge. The Federal guns reopened fire with destructive effect.[106]   Still, the Confederates came on.   Cooper's men noticed that a line of rebel infantry had crested on a hill just about 1,000 yards away coming right for them.   This was Wilcox's brigade in support of Pickett.   Cooper's and the other batteries trained their cannons on this new threat, first firing case shot and then, as the enemy got closer, double loads of canister.[107] One member of Wilcox's brigade recalled his experience:

For a few moments practically no loss occurred in our forward movement; but the Federal artillery soon got their range, and a storm of shot and shell was poured upon us. Shrapnel shot would burst in front of us and great gaps be made in our ranks, but the ranks would close and the line move forward....

At last we came within the range of grape and canister, and a hurricane of such missiles seemed to burst from a hundred cannon on our little line of about eight hundred, rank and file, and plow their deadly path through our ranks. We finally reached a scrubby timbered drain just under the enemy's position, and were passing through it as rapidly as possible when further participation, in so far as I was concerned, altogether ceased. A grape shot struck me down, and the struggle ended in so far as I was concerned. The retreat was ordered, and I was left alone to contemplate the horrors of war and the reckless and criminal folly of a military order which was subsequently repudiated by every officer from third lieutenant to the commanding general.[108]

The attack by Wilcox and Lang was ordered too late, and lacked coordination with Pickett. After the war, Wilcox indicated that Federal guns by themselves stopped him.[109] Many prisoners were brought in through Cooper's guns, and the field in his front was covered with the dead and wounded.[110] The Confederate assault, known more commonly as "Pickett's Charge," was thwarted and along with it Lee's hope to gain a victory in enemy territory.

For Cooper's men, July 3, while certainly not anti-climactic, did not result in as great a number of casualties as the other two days. Private Frederick Workman was slightly wounded in the arm.[111] On this day, the battery expended 150 rounds for a total of 1,050 over three days.[112]

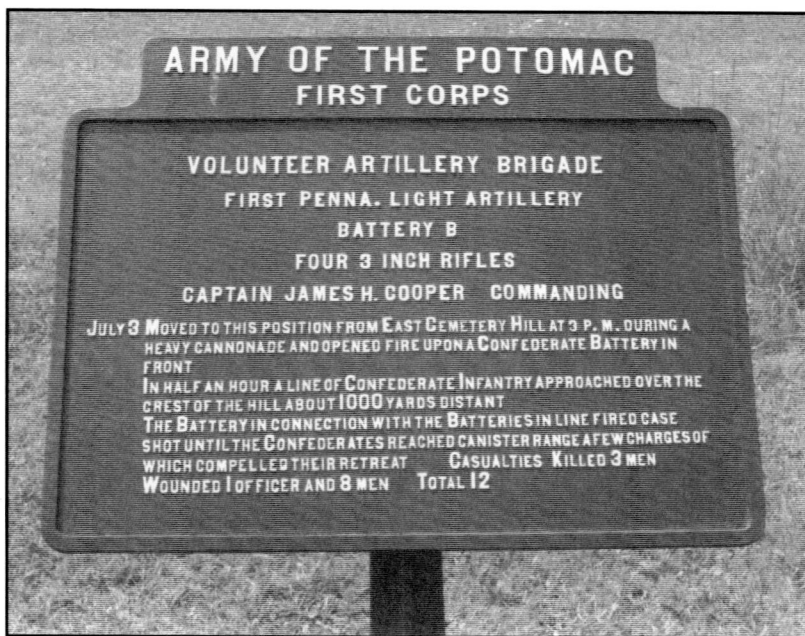

ARMY OF THE POTOMAC
FIRST CORPS

VOLUNTEER ARTILLERY BRIGADE
FIRST PENNA. LIGHT ARTILLERY
BATTERY B
FOUR 3 INCH RIFLES
CAPTAIN JAMES H. COOPER   COMMANDING

JULY 3 MOVED TO THIS POSITION FROM EAST CEMETERY HILL AT 3 P. M. DURING A HEAVY CANNONADE AND OPENED FIRE UPON A CONFEDERATE BATTERY IN FRONT
IN HALF AN HOUR A LINE OF CONFEDERATE INFANTRY APPROACHED OVER THE CREST OF THE HILL ABOUT 1000 YARDS DISTANT
THE BATTERY IN CONNECTION WITH THE BATTERIES IN LINE FIRED CASE SHOT UNTIL THE CONFEDERATES REACHED CANISTER RANGE A FEW CHARGES OF WHICH COMPELLED THEIR RETREAT   CASUALTIES KILLED 3 MEN
WOUNDED 1 OFFICER AND 8 MEN   TOTAL 12

National Park Service marker for Battery B's position on July 3. The battery was actually located further south on Cemetery Ridge. Also, contrary to the narrative on the marker, the battery moved to its position from the Artillery Reserve on that day rather than from East Cemetery Hill.

AFTERWARD

On the evening of July 1, James Alcorn trudged along the road toward Cashtown, a prisoner of war.[113] The following day he was paroled and started for Carlisle to be turned over to Federal authorities.[114] On the march, one of the rebel guards who happened to be a member of the Masonic fraternity took pity on him, a fellow Mason, and shared half of his three-day supply of rations with him. As Alcorn stated: "…his unselfish generosity can be better comprehended when the uncertainty of his getting anymore for himself is taken into consideration."[115]

James continued on along the road to Bendersville when he engaged a farmwoman in conversation who inquired about her two sons who were serving with the Pennsylvania Reserves. Even though he had no personal knowledge about their welfare, he assured her that they were safe which helped to ease his own burden after Alexander's death: "Poor old mother! While comforting her I seemed for the time, to feel the weight of my own great sorrow lift from my heart." The farmwoman gave James what appeared to be a half-bushel of cookies, and he bundled them up in his coat. As he ran to catch up with the guard, the sleeves loosened and the cookies began to fall out in the roadway. By that time he had lost over two-thirds of them, being devoured by both Federals and Confederates following behind him.[116]

Cemetery Gatehouse with post-battle additions on the right and rear. A path leads to the left to an area where Alexander P. Alcorn and James H. McCleary are buried.

James had high regard for his captors: "I cannot find it in my heart today to cherish any but the kindliest feelings for the rebel soldiers who guarded me on that occasion. Their treatment of the prisoners was kind and considerate in every particular, and their sorrow at my bereavement and to others was deep and heartfelt." He had praise for Brigadier General Fitzhugh Lee who had paroled him and who ordered that the prisoners be given good treatment which, if anything, was better than that afforded to the guards. He characterized the situation as more like being a guest than a prisoner, and to him Fitzhugh Lee, although a rebel, was "a brave and noble old man."[117]

Area of the Evergreen Cemetery where Alexander P. Alcorn and James H. McCleary are buried.

Arriving at Bendersville on July 3, James witnessed the hospitality of its inhabitants. On every street corner were people providing large amounts of bread, double spread with butter and apple butter, pies, cakes, fried chicken, and everything else that anyone could possibly want to eat. James noted: "The Bendersville people seemed to appreciate fully that the way to reach a soldier's heart was via his stomach."[118]

Between Bendersville and Papertown[119] the prisoners were formally turned over to Federal authorities, but James was not among them. Instead, he managed to slip away and left for Carlisle on his own. At about the same time that Cooper's battery was engaging the Confederates in their attack toward Cemetery Ridge at Gettysburg on July 3, James arrived in Carlisle. He ate four suppers and took up quarters in a vacant house without doors and windows where he did not get much rest: "The mosquitoes, it appeared, had also been on short rations and proposed to make the most of their opportunity." Being unable to sleep there, he got up and made his way to the market house where he met some fellow prisoners from the 14th Brooklyn Zouaves.[120] James had obtained a fine wool civilian hat the previous evening, the value of which was not known because James said: "The proprietor of the store was not present when I got it." He filled the spot where a Zouave had been lying and managed to fall asleep.[121]

Alexander P. Alcorn's grave site, Evergreen Cemetery, Gettysburg.

The following morning upon arising, James saw that his new hat was gone. He noted that in its place was the "greasiest, dirtiest old soldier cap that I ever saw." As he described it, the cap looked as though it had been used to carry bacon in for several months. He said: "I presume it served me right for having the hat in the first place, but at the time I was not in the mood for indulging in any moral reflection."[122]

On July 4, as the armies at Gettysburg rested from their ordeal, the parolees in Carlisle were being loaded into a train bound for parole camp, according to James, in Annapolis, Maryland.[123] James, though, was determined to go home. He had already telegraphed his father in Lawrence County and indicated that Alexander had been killed and that he was a prisoner, information he knew "…would nearly set my father and mother crazy." But he also realized that it would enable him to get home. What happened next was quite a remarkable experience.[124]

James was able to leave Carlisle without encountering the provost marshal and got to Harrisburg where he was to meet his father. Securing some new civilian clothes, he managed to escape detection by the provost guards. Just before that, he had actually

Grave marker of Peter G. Hoagland at the Soldier's National Cemetery, Gettysburg. Hoagland helped to carry James A. Alcorn's wounded brother to the Krauth House near the Seminary on July 1 and was himself mortally wounded the following day.

James H. McCleary's grave site, Evergreen Cemetery, Gettysburg.

Some members of the William P. Alcorn family and relatives. James is identified as the youngster directly in front of his mother while Alexander is standing in front of his father. Both hold the hands of Althena Alcorn, the grandmother of Ada-Marie Bowers who supplied the author with a colorized pre-war framed image from which this photograph was taken.

gone to Governor Curtin's Office at the Capitol and looked up the governor's private secretary, a personal acquaintance, whose influence enabled James to secure a pass to travel throughout the city. The secretary suggested that James go home and report to a Captain Culberson, the provost marshal of the district, who happened to be an individual James had saved during the Seven Days Battles in Virginia over a year earlier.[125]

On July 5, James' father arrived in Harrisburg with James S. Fullerton who served with the battery as a lieutenant until his discharge the preceding December and a neighbor and friend, John L. Hayes. They proceeded to Gettysburg to locate Alexander's remains and obtain information about any other members of the battery who had been killed or wounded. The trip to Carlisle from Harrisburg took three hours via train and once they arrived, the party could not secure any transportation to Gettysburg. They walked 15 miles to Bendersville, spending the night there, and for ten dollars managed to secure a horse team to take them to Gettysburg the next day.[126]

Once the group arrived at Gettysburg, they went looking for Alexander's gravesite near the Krauth house at the Seminary, but experienced some difficulty because the breastworks and trenches constructed by the Confederates had concealed the spot.[127] Eventually by accident they found it. Throughout the battlefield, James saw makeshift graves with arms and toes protruding above the ground after the recent rains washed away the loose ground covering them.[128]

Looking for the others elsewhere on the field who were killed, they were able to locate McCleary's body but not that of Hoagland. An army chaplain provided a funeral service for both men.[129] Today, the remains of Alexander Alcorn and James McCleary can be found buried in the Evergreen Cemetery adjacent to the Soldiers' National Cemetery where their graves are identified by individual markers with their names and unit identifications.

Three months after returning home, James was exchanged and resumed his place with the battery again. He was promoted to second lieutenant on April 8, 1864 and mustered out at the expiration of his term on November 23 of that year. James said when he enlisted he was only 19 years of age. He recalled plowing a cornfield on a bright April afternoon in 1861 and while deep in thought over his personal responsibility as a citizen of the republic, decided that it was time to act. After throwing the reins of the plow horse over the fence, he went to the house, got some personal items, saddled up his horse, and left for Mount Jackson where, in his words, "…I subscribed myself for three years, or during the war."[130]

After the war, James moved to Beaver, Pennsylvania for several years, trying his luck at oil development. Apparently, that was unsuccessful because he then moved to Crestline, Ohio, and then in 1870 to Bucyrus, Ohio, where he and his father operated a hotel. James must have been held in high esteem because he was appointed a special officer at the 1876 Centennial Exposition in Philadelphia and then a doorkeeper in the 47th Congress. After a fire destroyed the hotel, he relocated to Kinsley, Kansas for a fresh start where he again started a hotel business. In 1885, he married, but in less than a year, his first wife Mary died. On June 16, 1887, he married Louisa C. Muller from Pittsburgh, Pennsylvania. The couple had one daughter, Virginia.[131]

James H. Cooper in later life. Photograph taken from J.H. Stein's History of the Army of the Potomac (Washington: Gibson Bros., 1893), p. 470. The original positive glass plate is part of the A.W. Phipps Collection archived at the Lawrence County Historical Society, New Castle, Pennsylvania.

During his life in the west, James was described as a "pioneer," engaging in farming and raising cattle. Not willing to stay in any one place for long, he moved to Durango and Silverton, Colorado and then relocated to Missouri for a few years before returning to Kinsley. At one point, he was a postmaster as well as county coroner and held other positions of public trust.[132]

He died in Kinsley on January 21, 1911, leaving his wife and daughter.[133] He was buried at Hillside Cemetery with full honors accorded to him by the Masonic fraternity and the Grand Army of the Republic of which he had been a member.[134] For James Alcorn, who perhaps had never before ventured far away from home near Mount Jackson, his experience during the war at that age might have been responsible for his later desire to test his fortunes in a variety of occupations in different places. Freed psychologically from the local ties of his hometown by virtue of what he saw and did throughout his term of service, James was able to leave behind a life there that he might have otherwise pursued. In that sense, he was like many other veterans who moved west to make a new start, not content with remaining where they were before the war. Or perhaps his adventuresome spirit caused him to enlist in the first place. Either way, there is no question that he lived a diverse and interesting life.

On April 26, 1869, the members of Battery B held their first reunion in Nesbit Grove, Mount Jackson south of the old Methodist Episcopal Church. This was the month and day the battery was first organized.[135] In succeeding years, that date was first changed to June 8, when the battery entered state service, and then later June 28, when it was formally mustered in.[136] The reunions became a special day of celebration in Mount Jackson where ladies prepared food and flags decorated the homes. Beginning with a parade accompanied by the local band, the veterans would march to the picnic grounds, mount a platform decorated with bunting where they would conduct a business meeting, and then speakers would entertain the

Post-war photograph of Cooper, second from left, in front of Cooper and Butler's store on East Washington Street, New Castle, Pennsylvania.
(Courtesy of Emily Hoffman)

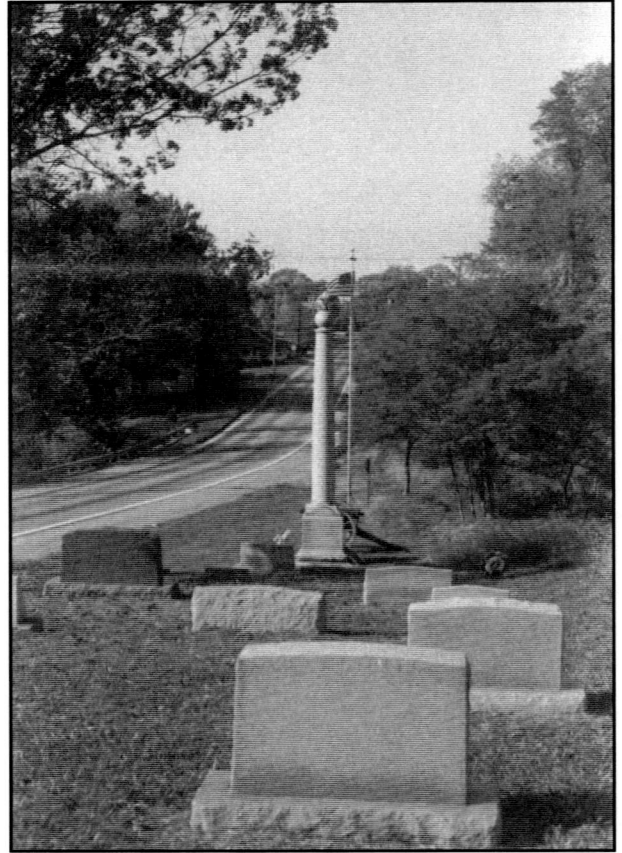

Monument to Battery B located along Route 108, Mount Jackson, Pennsylvania, from atop the knoll where the old Methodist Episcopal Church was located. Nesbit Woods, now Jackson Knolls, is to the left of the road.

audience who sat on plank seats. The crowd brought picnic baskets of food, and lemonade was available for all. During the evenings the entertainment would continue at the local churches and school.[137]

Among the first markers erected on the battlefield on land belonging to the Gettysburg Battlefield Memorial Association was a small octagonal granite column with a limestone die at the top. It was a marker to Cooper's Battery B and was placed near his position on East Cemetery Hill in 1880.[138]

On June 22, 1888 a contract was made between the Committee of Battery B, 1st Light Artillery PA Reserve Volunteer Corps and George W. Noll and N.F. Robinson, doing business as Noll & Robinson, for the construction of a larger monument to the battery that was to be placed on East Cemetery Hill near the old marker. The cost was $1,500.00.[139] James A. Gardner dedicated it on the field during Pennsylvania Day dedication ceremonies in Gettysburg on September 11, 1889.

In the intervening years, the people of Mount Jackson thought it appropriate to have a local monument to the battery erected there. Reverend Albert J. McCartney, a former pastor and later President of the Battery B Memorial Association, stated at the 1908 reunion: "I wish it generally understood that the proposed memorial is to be dedicated to all soldiers and not exclusively to Battery B although they and their friends are taking the initiative in raising the funds." Over a thousand dollars was raised or pledged

Marker first erected to Battery B on East Cemetery Hill.

Battery B monument on East Cemetery Hill.

that year, and the monument was completed in June, 1912 with only a balance of $270.00 needed. That amount was quickly raised at the reunion from the friends in attendance just before the dedication ceremonies.[140]

Just a month earlier, an agreement between the trustees and officers of the Battery B Memorial Association and the Methodist Episcopal Church permitted the erection of the monument on church grounds.[141] Everyone anxiously awaited its unveiling by Miss Mary Cooper, Cooper's daughter, which took place on June 28, 1912. Judge William E. Porter, then President of the Memorial Association, in his dedication address announced that it would be dedicated free from debt.[142]

The annual reunions continued throughout the years but, as expected, the ranks of the veterans thinned as time went on. The gatherings had moved to the Westfield Grange Hall, then the old Mount Jackson School, and finally the North Beaver Township School in Mount Jackson. On June 28, 1924, the Association marked 55 years of conducting reunions of Battery B. The year before at its business meeting, the members established a fund for the perpetual care of the plot of land, the local monument, and a gun provided by the government that was mounted on a carriage next to it. At that time, there was also interest in placing a marker for the battery on the field of the first day's battle.[143] This undertaking would not come into fruition until 1943, and after the Association ceased operations.

Solicitations were taken to secure $1,500.00 for the marker to be placed on South Reynolds Avenue where the battery occupied the first of its three positions held on that day.[144] This marker, which was the first since President Franklin D. Roosevelt dedicated the Eternal Light Peace Memorial in 1938, was

Battery B marker erected during World War II on South Reynolds Avenue where the battery first took up its position on July 1.

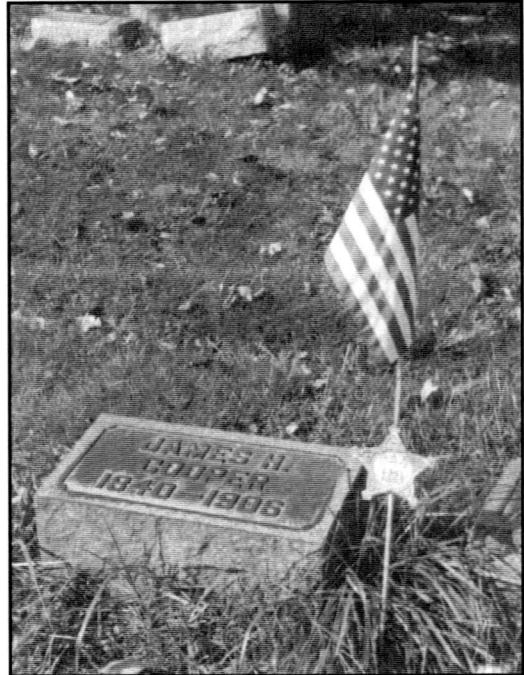

Grave of James H. Cooper, Greenwood Cemetery, New Castle, Pennsylvania.

Battery B veterans, probably at the reunion in Mount Jackson, Pennsylvania. James A. Gardner, Secretary of the organization, is standing in front, the first man on the left side. John M. Fullerton is standing second from the left in the row behind those seated on the platform.
(Courtesy of Nancy Gardner)

erected on July 24, 1943, and replaced an old wooden National Park Service one reciting the battery's service on July 1, 1863. The same inscription appeared on the new marker, but owing to the fact that World War II placed a demand on metal for the war effort, it was cut directly into the granite instead of on a bronze plaque.[145]

Among the former members of the battery, perhaps the one most instrumental in preserving the memory of its service was James A. Gardner. A schoolteacher at age 18 before the war, he enlisted in the battery as a private on July 24, 1861, and was mustered out as first lieutenant on June 9, 1865. After the war, he operated a store in the small community of Princeton and became involved in public service as a school board member and then justice of the peace.

Grave of James P. Alcorn and wife Louisa, Hillside Cemetery, Kinsley, Kansas.
(With permission of Kinsley Library web page. Photo by Mary Graff)

As a result of his experience with the law, Gardner decided to become a lawyer, and in 1876 was admitted to the Bar of Pennsylvania. In 1883 he became the solicitor for the city of New Castle, residing in the community with his wife, Mary, who he had married on August 11, 1865. The couple had four children One of his accomplishments was serving as a member of the convention that framed the municipal code governing third class cities in Pennsylvania. An expert in municipal law, he was active in the League of Third Class Cities in Pennsylvania and was known as the "father" of the League.

Gardner was the secretary of the Battery B Association for 50 years, and, as mentioned previously, gave the address at the battery's monument dedication at Gettysburg in 1889. He took a special interest in ascertaining the accurate position of the battery at Gettysburg, corresponding with Colonel John B. Bachelder who was involved with the Gettysburg Battlefield Memorial Association and Colonels John P. Nicholson and E.B. Cope. He died on May 24, 1925, at 82 years of age and was buried in Oak Park Cemetery in New Castle. [146]

Cooper exhibited great bravery during the war, being in the thick of action and having two horses shot out from under him on several occasions. On August 5, 1864, Generals Meade and Henry Hunt with

Grave of James A. Gardner, Oak Park Cemetery, New Castle, Pennsylvania

Colonel Wainwright recommended him to fill a vacant colonelcy which Cooper never formally presented to the War Department due to his modesty. [147] He also had declined Governor Curtin's offer of a major's commission in June of that year. His term of service having expired, Cooper left the battery on August 8, 1864.[148]

After the war, Cooper operated a lumber business, known as Hammond & Cooper.[149] He was part of the merchant tailoring firm of Cooper & Butler which operated on the main street of New Castle and dealt in men's clothing. He served as Sheriff of Lawrence County from 1874 to 1876, and participated in activities with the Association, serving as its president for a time. In the summer of 1905, Cooper attended the national convention of the Grand Army of the Republic in Denver, Colorado. At that time, it was discovered that he had heart disease. The following year, on March 21, 1906, at the age of 66 he died, only leaving a daughter as his survivor, his wife Alice having predeceased him. Just a week prior to his death, his sister died, leaving him as the last survivor of his immediate family. He was buried in Greenwood Cemetery in New Castle. Cooper was described as "extremely modest and retiring. Never exulted over his military record..."[150]

While readers of the Civil War tend to focus on the well-known personalities in the conflict, they often forget that the major accomplishments and acts of bravery come from the ordinary citizen-soldiers in the rank and file. Cooper, Gardner, and James Alcorn are illustrative of many men who served and afterward went about their personal lives with the satisfaction of knowing that their duty was accomplished. As Gardner stated at the dedication address for the battery's monument in Gettysburg:

> ....Having returned to our peaceful pursuits of life, we look back to the time when, upon this field and elsewhere, you were among the foremost men of this Nation; and right glad the people were then to have you foremost and front. You deserve and ought yet to be among the first in the hearts of this mighty people, who are richly enjoying the dearly bought privileges which your blood and your valor won.... Without the full measure of devotion which you unselfishly gave at the proper time and place, in the great extremity, we would not have this grand and glorious country of ours, of which we are this day so justly proud. In those eventful days we stood hand and hand, shoulder to shoulder, heart to heart, and fought upon many fields of bloody strife. Ties of friendship and association were then formed which nothing but the icy hand of death can destroy or tear asunder....
>
> Soon the cold hand of the destroyer will lay hold of you; and though your locks are becoming grey with fast declining years, though your steps are unsteady and your bodily infirmities are fast increasing, all caused by the hardships and privations of a cruel war; yet this we know—the fires of your lofty patriotism will continue to burn brightly to the end.[151]

For the veterans in attendance, Gardner's words must have caused some flashbacks to earlier times when they were mere youngsters, volunteering for service with great idealism. As they gazed around, they probably sensed that others who never directly tasted those privations of war could hardly appreciate the sacrifices that were made and the loss of fellow comrades as they did. The sun would set that day after the ceremonies were concluded, and the veterans would eventually depart for home. Afterward, only the memories of their mutually shared experiences would be available to sustain them.

Notes

[1] Harry W. Pfanz, Gettysburg-The First Day (Chapel Hill: The University of North Carolina Press, 2001), p. 123.

[2] Stephen M. Weld, War Diary and Letters of Stephen Minot Weld, 1861-1865 (Cambridge, Massachusettes: Riverside Press, 1912), p. 230; George Meade, Life and Letters of George Gordon Meade, Vol. 2 (New York: Chas. Scribner's Sons, 1913), p. 36. Cooper's battery just became attached to Biddle's brigade on July 1. See: James and Judy McLean, Gettysburg Sources, Vol. 3 (Baltimore: Butternut and Blue, 1990), p. 109.

[3] Allan Nevins (ed.), A Diary of Battle: The Personal Journals of Colonel Charles S. Wainwright, 1861-1865 (New York: Harcourt, Brace & World, 1962), p. 233.

4 Times are only approximate. The reports vary in that regard. See: O.R. Vol. 27.1, pp. 312, 315, 319-320, 327. Edwin Coddington, a reputed authority on the battle, maintained that the brigade arrived between 11:00 a.m. and noon. Edwin B. Coddington, The Gettysburg Campaign, A Study in Command (Dayton, Ohio: Morningside Bookshop, 1983), p. 279. Warren W. Hassler, Jr., another historian, suggested its arrival to be about 11:15 a.m. or perhaps a little later. Warren W. Hassler, Jr., Crisis at the Crossroads (University, Alabama: University of Alabama Press, 1970), pp. 55-56. Cooper's battery marker on South Reynolds Avenue states that it went into position at noon.

5 For the classic history of the Iron Brigade generally, see Alan T. Nolan, The Iron Brigade (Reprinted ed., Berrien Springs, Michigan: Hardscrabble Books, 1983). Also see Lance J. Herdegen, The Men Stood Like Iron: How the Iron Brigade Got Its Name (Bloomington: Indiana University Press, 1997). Herbst Woods has often been referred to as McPherson's Woods and Reynolds' Woods.

6 O.R. Vol. 27.1, pp. 317, 320; Michael A. Dreese, The 151st Pennsylvania Volunteers at Gettysburg, Like Ripe Apples in a Storm (Jefferson, North Carolina: McFarland & Company, Inc., 2000), p. 38.

7 O.R. Vol. 27.1, pp. 315, 317, 320; Pfanz, Gettysburg-The First Day, p. 128; Hassler, pp. 57-58. According to David G. Martin in Gettysburg July 1 (Cambridge, Massachusettes: DeCapo Press, 2003), p. 181, on their return back, Biddle's men did not occupy the reverse slope but were in front of Cooper's guns, fully exposed at the order of General Wadsworth to discourage any Confederate attack in that sector. This edition of Martin's book contains revisions made since its original publication in 1995.

8 O.R. Vol. 27.1, pp. 313, 315. Cooper's position on the ridge was described as an oat field between 350—380 yards south of the Chambersburg (Cashtown) Road. O.R. Vol. 27.1, pp. 229, 355. The E.B. Cope Map, NMP-Get-8447, Gettysburg National Military Park Library [hereinafter referred to as GNMPL], purportedly had marked the field conditions during he battle but does not show an oat field there. The distance, though, is substantially correct. Biddle's line is marked by South Reynolds Avenue today. Wainwright stated that he placed Cooper's battery there and ordered him to await events. Nevins, p. 234. Cooper's guns at Gettysburg were not those he originally had earlier in the war. See: Stephen W. Sears, To the Gates of Richmond (New York: Ticknor & Fields, 1992), p. 296; Bates, History of the PA Volunteers, Vol. 1, p. 949. Martin, pp. 593-594 has a listing of guns used by the batteries at Gettysburg on the first day. See also: George W. Newton, Silent Sentinels (New York: Savas Beatie, LLC, 2005), p. 153.

9 O.R. Vol. 27.1, p. 247, 295, 299, 301; Ken Bandy, et al., Gettysburg Papers, Vol. 1 (Dayton, Ohio: Morningside Bookshop, 1978), 296. Doubleday took credit for having the breastworks constructed. Abner Doubleday, Chancellorsville and Gettysburg (New York: Chas. Scribner's Sons, 1882), p. 147. When Henry Baxter's Second Brigade came up, it also added to the breastworks begun by Paul's men. Martin, pp. 185-186. The barricade was at the foot of the ridge below the Seminary, facing west.

10 O.R. 27.1, p. 327. Compare: Hassler, p. 57. Hassler suggested that the 151st Pennsylvania was initially detached and left at the Seminary while the official report of Lieutenant Colonel McFarland stated that the regiment was not detached until 2:00 p.m. Martin, p. 181, has the regiment on Biddle's line at McPherson Ridge during the noontime lull. It was located on the right of Biddle's line near the southeast corner of Herbst Woods. Dreese, The 151st Pennsylvania Volunteers at Gettysburg, p. 38.

11 For Wainwright's version see O.R. Vol. 27.1, p. 356; Nevins, p. 232. Stewart claimed he told Wadsworth he would post his battery near the railroad cut. Bandy, et al., Vol. 1, p. 368. Pfanz, Gettysburg-The First Day, p. 128 chose Wainwright's recitation that he directed Stewart to remain south of the seminary.

12 Nevins, p. 234.

13 Ibid. On May 12, 1863, General Hooker, who had commanded the Army of the Potomac previously, issued an order consolidating the batteries into brigades with each corps having one under the control of the chief of artillery for that corps. This would allow the artillery to function in a more efficient and coordinated manner rather than being parceled out under the control of different infantry commanders all over the field at their own discretion. See: Bert Barnett, "Union Artillery on July 3," Mr. Lincoln's Army, The Army of the Potomac in the Gettysburg Campaign (Programs of the 6th Annual Gettysburg Seminar—GNMP, The Natl. Park Service, 1997), pp. 212-214. This idea was originally conceived by Wainwright months earlier. Ibid., p. 212; Nevins, p. 114.

14 O.R. Vol. 27.1, pp. 355-356; Martin, pp. 191, 193.

15 Hassler, p. 59.

16 O.R. Vol. 27.1, pp. 315, 317. This was the Harmon Farm. See: Martin, pp. 182-183.

17 O.R. Vol. 27.1, p. 365. In his recollections of the battle 25 years afterward, James P. Alcorn stated that a solid shot struck the handspike of one gun but did no damage except to the seat of the pants of several gunners. But the gun that he said was damaged and sent to the rear for repairs he attributed to a shot from a rebel battery. See: Transcription of Recollections of James P. Alcorn, GNMPL.

18 O.R. Vol. 27.1, p. 364; Nicholson, p. 878.

19 Pfanz, Gettysburg-The First Day, p. 156.

20 O.R. Vol. 27.1, p. 364; Nicholson, p. 878.

21 O.R. Vol. 27.1, pp. 248, 315, 317, 320, 327.

22 Nicholson, p. 878; O.R. Vol. 27.1, p. 356; Pfanz, Gettysburg-The First Day, p. 157.

23 Nicholson, Ibid. Case shot was a hollow-like projectile that was filled with smaller balls held together with melted sulfur or resin and containing a powder charge. When the projectile was fired from the cannon, a timed fuse that had been inserted into it was ignited from the combustion inside the tube. At the pre-arranged distance, the fuse would detonate and the shell and its contents would spray out, usually above the target. See: L. VanLoan Naisawald, Grape and Canister (Reprinted ed., Gaithersburg, Maryland: Old Soldier Books, Inc., [n.d.]), pp. 537-552 for a discussion of artillery types and projectiles. For a detailed study of field artillery generally, see: Philip M. Cole, Civil War Artillery at Gettysburg, (Orrtanna, Pennsylvania: Colecraft Industries, 2002).

24 Nicholson, Ibid.; Martin, p. 240.

25 O.R. Vol. 27.1, p. 364. James A. Gardner who served with the battery stated that Wainwright's order relocating the battery from its second position came at 3:00 p.m. Nicholson, p. 878. In a letter to Colonel E. B. Cope, Commissioner and Superintendent of the Battlefield, on March 2, 1923, Gardner acknowledged reading Cooper's report but insisted that the battery was actually there for at least an hour and a half and not a few minutes. Given the fact that only 25 rounds were fired from Cooper's first position and Cooper reported firing a total of 400 that day, then 375 were fired from the other two positions occupied by the three guns of the battery. See: Gardner's letter, GNMPL. Pfanz, Gettysburg-The First Day, p. 157, maintained that Cooper's and Reynolds' batteries were contending with Rodes for about an hour.

26 Pfanz, Gettysburg-The First Day, pp. 136-137; Hassler, pp. 66, 68. General Reynolds is said to have first appreciated the strategic importance of Cemetery Hill. Samuel P. Bates, The Battle of Gettysburg (Reprinted, Gaithersburg, Maryland: Ron R. VanSickle Military Books, 1987), p. 75. See also: Edward J. Nichols, Toward Gettysburg, a Biography of General John F. Reynolds (Reprinted, Gaithersburg, Maryland: Butternut Press, Inc., 1986), p. 255, nt. 67. But it was Howard who took steps to occupy it with General Steinwehr's division of the Eleventh Corps.

27 See generally: David L. Valuska and Christian B. Keller, Damn Dutch, Pennsylvania Germans at Gettysburg (Mechanicsville, Pennsylvania: Stackpole Books, 2004).

28 Nevins, p. 235; O.R. Vol. 27.1, p. 356. According to Wadsworth's report, though, Howard had given direct orders to him to hold "Seminary Ridge as long as possible." O.R. Vol. 27.1, p. 266. Coddington indicated that Hancock did not arrive until between 4:00 and 4:30 p.m. when the Federal troops had already been withdrawing to Cemetery Hill. Coddington, p. 297. Martin suggested that Hancock arrived about 4:30 p.m. and witnessed the retreat that was already in progress. Martin, p. 483. Hancock himself stated that he arrived at 3:00 p.m. O.R., Vol. 27.1, p. 368. But Martin felt Hancock's estimate was too early. See: Martin, p. 683, nt. 83; Bandy, et al., Vol. 1, pp. 331-333, 335. Howard and Doubleday maintained that Hancock arrived at 4:30 p.m. O.R. Vol. 27.1, p. 704; Doubleday, pp. 150-151. With the weight of authority putting Hancock's arrival at 4:30 p.m. when the retreat was already in progress, it is hard to imagine how Wainwright could suggest that Hancock ordered Cemetery Hill to be held at all hazards when Hancock had not yet arrived on the field. Martin accepted the portion of Wainwright's rendition that he overheard the aide tell Doubleday to hold Cemetery Hill which Wainwright interpreted to be Seminary Hill. Martin, p. 349. But Martin did not comment on the other part of Wainwright's story that it was Hancock who purportedly had issued the order. Martin, Ibid.

29 O.R. Vol. 27.1, pp. 327-328; Hassler, pp. 111-115 details the Federal withdrawal from McPherson Ridge.

30 O.R. Vol. 27.1, p. 356; Nicholson, p. 878; Letter of James A. Gardner to Colonel E.B. Cope dated March 2, 1923, GNMPL; Martin credited Howard with ordering Cooper from the meadow to Seminary Ridge. Martin, p. 349. But this conclusion is not supported by his citations on that point. See: Martin, p. 662, nt. 38. In fact, he cited Wainwright's report and journal, both of which indicated that Wainwright placed Cooper at the Seminary. Pfanz maintained that Wainwright ordered Cooper to Seminary Ridge. Pfanz, Gettysburg-The First Day, p. 297. Howard's battle report made no mention of him placing Cooper's battery, O.R. Vol. 27.1, pp. 701-707. Wainwright's reference to the "professor's house" in his report was undoubtedly Rev. Dr. Charles Philip Krauth's home.

31 Nicholson, pp. 878-879; Martin, p. 397; Pfanz, Gettysburg-The First Day, p. 297. This new attack on Stone was again made by Junius Daniel's brigade.

32 Nicholson, p. 879; Martin, p. 397.

33 Perrin's and Scales' brigades were part of Major General William D. Pender's division of Hill's Corps. Brigadier General James H. Lane's brigade, also part of Pender's division, attacked further south where Buford's cavalry was positioned along Seminary Ridge south of the Fairfield Road.

34 Maine at Gettysburg: Report of Maine Commissioners (Portland: Lakeside Press, 1898), p. 84; Martin, p. 397.

35 O.R. Vol. 27.1, pp 356, 364; Nicholson, p. 878; Pfanz, Gettysburg-The First Day, p. 297. Pfanz disputed this in nt. 8, p. 425.

36 Wadsworth authorized the placement of Stewart's battery. Wainwright was unaware that others had posted Stevens' and Stewart's batteries as he was preoccupied with Cooper's and Reynolds' guns. See: Nevins, p. 235. While Wilbur's section of Reynolds' (now Breck's) battery was on Stevens' right with one gun actually on the Chambersburg Pike, Reynolds' other guns under the command of Lieutenant William H. Bower which were pulled back from McPherson Ridge were located behind a stone wall on Seminary Ridge south of the buildings and near the Fairfield Road. O.R. Vol. 27.1, pp. 356, 362-363.

  According to James A. Gardner, Cooper's and Stevens' batteries were located further down the slope from the Seminary buildings (specifically the Krauth House) near the northwest corner of a woodlot. This is further west than the position marked by Steven's guns today. See: Letter of Gardner to Colonel John P. Nicholson, Secretary of Pennsylvania Monument Commission, dated October 22, 1902, GNMPL. But Colonel William W. Robinson of the Seventh Wisconsin stated that when his men arrived at the foot of Seminary Ridge, they occupied the loose rail breastworks which were 40 yards in front of a battery. O.R. Vol. 27.1, p. 280. Given the placement of the breastworks 40 yards in front of the battery, Cooper's and Stevens' guns had to be further up on the ridge and not in the northwest corner of the woodlot. Also in his address at the dedication of the battery's monument on September 11, 1889, Gardner stated that Cooper had the infantry at the barricade in the battery's immediate front cleared so that the guns could fire slightly to the left at Perrin's brigade. Nicholson, p. 879.

37 O.R. Vol. 27.1, pp. 356-357.

38 O.R. 27.1, p. 364; David L. and Audry J. Ladd, editors, The Bachelder Papers, Vol. 3 (Dayton, Ohio: Morningside Press, 1995), pp. 1620-1621; Nicholson, p. 879. Undoubtedly, Davison's section, firing obliquely across the Chambersburg Pike, created the most damage to Scales' left. O.R. Vol. 27.1, p. 357. Canister was basically a metal container filled with smaller balls that was most effective against attacking infantry at close range. Once the container ruptured upon detonation within the barrel, the balls would immediately spray out.

39 Maine at Gettysburg, p. 84.

40 O.R. Vol. 27.1, p. 280.

41 J. Michael Miller, "Perrin's Brigade on July 1, 1863," Gettysburg Magazine, (Issue 13), p. 27. Miller presents a detailed account of the fighting at the Seminary.

42 Nicholson, p. 879. There is some speculation as to whom the color bearer belonged. James A. Gardner thought him to possibly be of the 13th South Carolina. Ladd & Ladd, Vol. 3, pp. 1620-1621. Gardner, however, was incorrect because the 13th South Carolina occupied Perrin's extreme right near the Fairfield Road, far south from Cooper's guns. That unit along with 12th South Carolina had made an oblique to the right to engage cavalry south of the road but did not change position from the left of the 14th South Carolina as Gardner had assumed based on his interpretation of Perrin's report. The color bearer was probably from the 14th South Carolina. There is also a reference to a color bearer placing the colors on the breastworks in front of Cooper's battery as it was leaving Seminary Ridge. See: Nevins, p. 236; Pfanz, Gettysburg-The First Day, p. 313.

43 Varina Davis Brown, A Colonel at Gettysburg and Spotsylvania (Columbia, South Carolina: State Company, 1931), p. 80.

44 O.R. Vol. 27.2, p. 662.

45 Ibid. See also Pfanz, Gettysburg-The First Day, p. 312. There is one account suggesting that a physical obstruction, a post and board fence running obliquely in the front of the right wing of the 1st South Carolina, actually caused the regiment to veer left. Martin, p. 408.

46 O.R. Vol. 27.1, pp. 318, 321, 323, 364; Nicholson, p. 879-880.

47 Pfanz, Gettysburg-The First Day, p. 312.

48 O.R. Vol. 27.1, p. 357; Nevins, p. 236. Lieutenant Colonel Alfred B. McCalmont of the 142nd Pennsylvania had warned Cooper that the infantry on the left south of the Seminary building had gone and that unless he withdrew immediately, he would be captured. Nicholson, pp. 879-880. According to James A. Gardner, this prompted Cooper to limber up to the rear. Fortunately, Cooper had already ordered full limbers and sent out the caissons to Cemetery Hill. Nicholson, p. 880. A limber was a two-wheeled vehicle having an ammunition chest on top. The cannon was attached to the rear of the limber, and both the limber and attached gun were pulled by a team of six horses. A caisson, also two-wheeled, had two ammunition chests together with a spare wheel on the back. It carried a spare pole. The caisson was attached to the rear of its own limber and both were likewise pulled by a team of six horses. A battery would have a limber/caisson for each limber/gun.

49 Ladd & Ladd, Vol. 3, p. 1939

50 Maine at Gettysburg, p. 88. While limbering up, Stevens' gunners sustained several casualties from rebel fire. As the battery departed and moved toward the town, a wheel fell off one of the cannons, forcing the men to halt and replace it while pressed by the enemy. Ibid., p. 86. One gun in Lieutenant Wilbur's section of Reynolds' battery was abandoned when four horses were shot down as they were leaving. Ibid., pp. 85-86; O.R. Vol. 27.1, p. 357; Nevins, p. 237; Doubleday, p. 149. According to Stewart, an axle on one of his caissons broke and, with four horses killed, was abandoned. A cannoneer stayed behind to destroy the powder bags. Bandy, et al., Vol. 1, pp. 372-373. In his report, Wainwright indicated that one of Stewart's caissons was blown up by enemy fire, and a total of three others had to be abandoned. O.R., Vol. 27.1, p. 357; See also Maine at

Gettysburg, p. 86. The one referred to by Stewart is probably one of those three. Another version had one of the caissons of Stewart's Battery B lose a wheel. The artilleryman jacked up the caisson, replaced the wheel, and resumed the march. See: C.V. Tevis and D.R. Marquis, History of the Fighting Fourteenth (Reprinted ed., Baltimore: Butternut and Blue, 1994), p. 87. One of Stewart's guns had also been damaged, and while it was being repaired, two other guns held off the pursuing Confederates. Bandy, et al., Vol. 1, p. 371. Unknown to Stewart until later, Davison had been severely wounded and was in one of the hospitals. Ibid., p. 373. Sergeant Mitchell of that section of the battery had taken over the responsibility of drawing off the guns. Martin, pp. 432, 443.

[51] O.R., Vol. 27.1, p. 357; Nevins, p. 236.

[52] This maneuver brought the limber around in a loop so that its rear faced the rear of the gun for attachment. Instruction for Field Artillery 1864 (Reprinted ed., New Market, Virginia: John M. Bracken, 1994), p. 160, No. 420.

[53] Recollections of James P. Alcorn, Ibid.

[54] Ibid.

[55] Ibid. Alcorn identified the building where his brother was brought as Dr. Croft's house. The battery was located near Dr. Krauth's residence north of the Seminary building. It was a brick house, served as a hospital, and was probably the premises referred to by Alcorn. See: Michael A. Dreese, The Hospital on Seminary Ridge at the Battle of Gettysburg, (Jefferson, North Carolina: McFarland & Company, Inc., 2002), pp. 73, 89. James stated that his brother died the following evening which would have been July 2. But he later indicated that he had been marched out toward Cashtown with other prisoners and was paroled at about 5:00 p.m. on July 2. Therefore, Alexander died on the evening of July 1 rather than the following evening because James had buried him before he left with the other prisoners.

[56] According to Wainwright, there were 83 casualties and 80 horses killed for all of his batteries. O.R. Vol. 27.1, p. 357.

[57] The wounded men included Lieutenant William C. Miller and Privates John W. Phillips, John Pauly, and Asahel Shaffer. O.R. Vol. 27.1, p. 365; Nicholson, p. 880. The complete casualty list showed that Miller was wounded in the left shoulder slightly, Phillips and Pauly were wounded in the arm severely, and Shaffer was wounded in the arm slightly. Two horses were also killed. James Alcorn was listed as prisoner and his brother, Alexander, was said to have been wounded in the left thigh seriously and a prisoner. See: Casualty List of July 1, 1863, GNMPL

[58] Nicholson, p. 880. Ames commanded an Eleventh Corps' brigade and then assumed command of the First Division of that corps when Brigadier General Francis C. Barlow was wounded.

[59] Cooper's guns were placed in this position by order of Wainwright. O.R. Vol. 27.1, p. 365. Cooper's lunettes were not completed until the following morning. Nicholson, p. 880. According to Biddle in an address before the Historical Society of Pennsylvania on March 8, 1880, when Hancock arrived he found nothing special about the works on East Cemetery Hill. All that was constructed at that time were "some holes (not deep) dug to sink the wheels and trains of the pieces." GNMPL, Archival Box Coll., B-32, p. 42; McLean, p. 121. Captain R. Bruce Ricketts, whose battery relieved Cooper's late on July 2, stated that small lunettes were thrown up for each gun but offered little protection. Wiedrich's battery had similar ones. Ladd & Ladd, Vol. 2, pp. 1172-1173. But a post-battle photograph of Stewart's gun emplacements shows earth and rail barricades which were more than mere shallow holes. See: William A. Frassanito, Gettysburg, A Journey in Time (New York: Chas. Scribner's Sons, 1975), p. 115. Since Hancock had yet to place Stewart's battery when he arrived, the construction of the Stewart's lunettes might not have even begun when he made his observations. The East Cemetery Hill lunettes visible today had been altered over the years. See nt. 63, infra.

[60] Edward N. Whittier, "The Left Attack (Ewell's) at Gettysburg," Massachusettes MOLLUS, reprinted in Bandy, et al., Vol. 2 pp. 757-794. See also: Colonel James K.P. Scott, The Story of the Battles at Gettysburg (Harrisburg: The Telegraph Press, 1927), p. 220. Another account presents an entirely different rendition of what occurred. See: Maine at Gettysburg, pp. 88-89. According to that writer, Hancock called out for the captain of "that brass battery" which was located near the cemetery gatehouse. When Stevens approached Hancock, the latter pointed to Culp's Hill and ordered Stevens to take his battery there and "stop the enemy from coming up that ravine." See also: Pfanz, Gettysburg-The First Day, pp. 335-336.

[61] Meade originally considered fighting along Pipe Creek.

[62] Nevins, p. 237. Major Thomas W. Osborn of the Eleventh Corps artillery indicated that there was really a division of control between himself and Wainwright as to the batteries on Cemetery Hill and that he got his orders from Howard directly. Martin, p. 475.

[63] Martin, Ibid. According to Stewart, General Hancock told him where to place his guns. Bandy, et al., p. 373. But the location is unclear. Wainwright stated that four of Stewart's gun faced northwest along the pike, and another section was between Cooper and Breck. Nevins, p. 238. But two of Stewart's guns had been disabled in the retreat. Therefore, Wainwright was incorrect in his journal entry as to the number of guns. In his official report, however, Wainwright acknowledged that two of Stewart's guns were disabled, but that all four of the others faced the town. O.R. Vol. 27.1, p. 357. See also Harry W. Pfanz, Gettysburg-Culp's Hill & Cemetery Hill (Chapel Hill: University of North Carolina Press, 1993), p. 170. Pfanz also indicated

that Stewart's guns were placed there by Wainwright rather than Hancock. The battlefield tablet for Stewart's battery on East Cemetery Hill states that of the four guns which were in operation, two were on the pike and the other two were in the field. Stewart noted that when Hancock asked him how many serviceable guns he had, Stewart replied four. Hancock ordered him to place three along the pike facing the town and one at right angles to them and not move them except by his order. Stewart stated that he remained in that position until July 4. Bandy, et al., pp. 373-374; Martin, p. 681, nt. 38. While Martin accepted this scenario in nt. 38, his text maintained that three guns faced northwest to fire down the road and a section (two guns) faced east between Cooper and Breck. Martin, p. 475. This would indicate the presence of five guns rather than four.

William A. Frassanito in his photographic study of the field was admittedly unable to locate the exact positions of the batteries from post-war photographs of the lunettes that existed there. The lunettes had been reconstructed years after the battle and did not represent what appeared on the field at that time. See: William A. Frassanito, Early Photography at Gettysburg (Gettysburg: Thomas Publications, 1995), p. 145. In fact, several had been obliterated or were larger than originally prepared. Ladd & Ladd, Vol. 2, p. 982, 1172. But Frassanito's work also shows photographs of the area occupied by Stewart taken just days after the battle which depict the remains of three lunettes on one side of the pike and one on the other, all facing northwest toward the town. Frassanito, Early Photography at Gettysburg, pp. 140-141, 164. Yet he suggested that perhaps two of Stewart's guns faced east behind several lunettes there but were shifted to the other positions facing northwest, meaning that Stewart constructed six lunettes for four cannons. Ibid., pp. 145, 416 nt. 7 (East Cemetery Hill-GBMA (51)). Stewart, himself, recalled that his guns did not change position. Thus, the sources and the physical remains of the lunettes are not consistent in ascertaining Stewart's placement. Accepting Stewart's recollection, three guns faced northwest on the pike and one was located perpendicular to them facing east. When reconciling this with the physical remains immediately after the battle, another possibility is that Stewart's men constructed four lunettes facing northwest with the expectation that the one gun facing east would eventually join the other three along the pike.

[64] Martin, p. 476.

[65] O.R. Vol. 27.1, pp. 358, 365; Nicholson, pp. 880-881; Pfanz, Culp's Hill and Cemetery Hill, p. 178.

[66] Nicholson, p. 881; Pfanz, Culp's Hill and Cemetery Hill, p. 170.

[67] Nicholson, Ibid.; Pfanz, Culp's Hill and Cemetery Hill, pp. 170-171.

[68] Another advantage of the smoothbore 12-pound Napoleon gun was that it was faster to load because the ammunition was "fixed," the powder bag already being attached to the projectile by means of a wooden sabot. It is no wonder that Hancock wanted Stevens' guns on the slope of Culp's Hill to sweep the ravine in the event of a Confederate attack there and also have Stewart's guns facing the town to stop any infantry threat from that direction. For a detailed discussion of fighting methods and weapons during the Civil War, including artillery, see Brent Nosworthy, The Bloody Crucible of Courage (New York: Carroll & Graf, 2003) and Paddy Griffith, Battle Tactics of the Civil War (New Haven: Yale University Press, 1989). An introduction to military tactics can also be found in Grady M. McWhiney and Perry D. Jamieson, Attack and Die, Civil War Military Tactics and the Southern Heritage (University, Alabama: The University of Alabama Press, 1982).

[69] Pfanz, Culp's Hill and Cemetery Hill, p. 171.

[70] Nicholson, p. 881; Pfanz, Culp's Hill and Cemetery Hill, p. 179. The Parrott guns which were rifled and fired conical projectiles, were originally developed by Robert P. Parrott of the West Point Foundry in 1861. Copies were made by the Confederates. Unlike the Ordnance Rifles with wrought iron tubes, the barrels on the Parrotts were made of more fragile cast iron which were easier to manufacture. To compensate for the inherent structural weakness of cast iron, the breech end of the barrel, which was most susceptible to rupture, had a reinforcing collar made of wrought iron. Cooper had 10-pound Parrotts earlier in the war.

[71] Nicholson, Ibid.

[72] From Pfanz, Culp's Hill and Cemetery Hill, p. 180. Used by permission of publisher; Thomas W. Osborn, "The Artillery at Gettysburg," Philadelphia Weekly Times , May 31, 1879.

[73] Bandy, et al., pp. 374-375.

[74] Nevins, p. 243; Nicholson, p. 881.

[75] Nicholson, Ibid.

[76] Ibid. Cooper's report indicated that the bombardment consumed 2 1/2 hours before the Confederate guns were silenced. O.R., Vol. 27.1, p. 365. Wainwright's report stated it took about 1 1/2 hours. O.R., Vol. 27.1, p. 358. But in his journal, Wainwright said it took about 2 hours. Nevins, p. 243. Lieutenant Whittier of Stevens' battery said the enemy batteries on Benner's Hill were silenced in a half hour. Maine at Gettysburg, p. 93.

[77] Nevins, pp. 243-244. Wainwright also carelessly walked in the way of the muzzle of one of Breck's guns as it was about to fire.

[78] Nevins, p. 244.

[79] Ibid., p. 243. See discussion: "Some Unanswered Questions" infra. for a critique of Wainwright's recollection of this incident.

80 Ibid. Wainwright was critical of Cooper's tolerance toward stragglers in his battery while enroute to Gettysburg. Ibid., pp. 219-220. Cooper was more lenient; as long as the men showed up in camp for roll call, he did not care that they strayed away from their detachment while on the march.

81 Nevins, p. 243.

82 Nicholson, p. 882.

83 Pfanz, Culp's Hill and Cemetery Hill, p 185.

84 Nicholson, p. 882.

85 Pfanz, Culp's Hill and Cemetery Hill, pp. 186-187.

86 O.R. Vol. 27.1, p. 358

87 O.R. Vol. 27.1, p. 363

88 Ibid.

89 O.R. Vol. 27.1, pp. 358, 365; Pfanz, Culp's Hill and Cemetery Hill, pp. 252-253. There is some dispute by Ricketts as to when he arrived to relieve Cooper. He claimed to have relieved him at 4:00 p.m. or no later than 4:30 p.m. See: Ladd & Ladd, Vol. 1, pp. 600-601; Vol. 2, pp. 972-973, 981, 982,1172. See also Letter of Lieutenant C.E. Brockway (Battery F, 1st PA Artillery) to D. McConaughy dated March 5, 1864. Battery F Papers, Brake Collection, U.S. Military History Institute, Ridgway Hall, Carlisle, PA.

90 O.R. Vol. 27.1, p. 365; Nicholson, p. 882. James A. Gardner felt that the amount of ammunition expended was indicative of how long the battery was actually in position during the artillery duel. Ladd & Ladd, p. 1622; Nicholson, p. 882.

91 John W. Busey, The Last Full Measure (Hightstown, New Jersey: Longstreet House,1988), pp. 137, 168. Cooper's official report lists both as killed. O.R. Vol. 27.1, p. 365. So does the casualty list for July 2, 1863. See: GNMPL.

92 Casualty List of July 2, 1863, Ibid. The other wounded included Privates Daniel W. Taylor, wounded slightly in the arm; James C. Cornelius, wounded slightly in the right jaw; and Corporal Joseph Reed. Casualty List of July 2, 1863, Ibid. O.R. Vol. 27.1, p. 365; Nicholson, p. 882.

93 Casualty List of July 2, 1863, Ibid.

94 O.R. Vol. 27.1, p. 365. Cooper's report stated that after going to the Artillery Reserve, he was ready for action at 11:00 a.m., but not receiving any orders, the battery stayed there until the following day. Obviously, since the battery did not go into reserve until the evening of July 2, Cooper meant that he stayed in reserve into the following day and was ready for action at 11:00 a.m. which would have been July 3. James A. Gardner stated that the disabled gun was repaired and the battery was ready for duty at 11:00 a.m. on the following day, being July 3. Nicholson, p. 882. The Artillery Reserve position was south of the Granite Schoolhouse Lane which led to the Taneytown Road from the Baltimore Pike. It was reached by turning right from the Baltimore Pike onto the lane at Power's Hill.

95 Captain James Stewart had suggested that when Ewell made his assault on East Cemetery Hill, a Louisiana Tiger infantryman of General Early's division was captured by one of Cooper's men. Bandy, et al., p. 375. This was, obviously, in error since Cooper's battery was not there during that assault.

96 One historian suggested that General Lee's plan was to attack Cemetery Hill and not the center of the Federal position on Cemetery Ridge. He contended that Lee's intention for July 3 was merely the continuation of a plan to drive the Federals off Cemetery Hill that existed the day before when he proposed his en echelon attack on the Federal left. See: Troy D. Harmon, Lee's Real Plan at Gettysburg (Mechanicsburg, Pennsylvania: Stackpole Books, 2003). Harmon's thesis was originally presented in his book, Cemetery Hill "The general plan was unchanged" (Baltimore: Butternut and Blue, 2001).

97 Earl J. Hess, Pickett's Charge—The Last Attack at Gettysburg (Chapel Hill: The University of North Carolina Press, 2001), p. 117. Estimates vary. Compare: Coddington, p. 486. His figure is between 170-179 guns.

98 Ibid., p. 76.

99 Ibid., pp. 113-114. Hess opined that McGilvery had a total of 39 guns. General Hunt's report of the guns in McGilvery's line prior to Cooper coming into position shows 33. Accepting General Hunt's report, the batteries comprising McGilvery's line were arranged as follows: From the north and running south, Thompson's Batteries C and F, 1st Pennsylvania (five 3-inch rifles), Phillips' Battery F, 5th Massachusetts (six 3-inch rifles), Hart's 15th New York (four 12-pound Napoleons), Sterling's 2nd Connecticut (four James guns and two howitzers), Rank's 3rd Pennsylvania Heavy Artillery section (two 3-inch rifles) Dow's Battery F, 6th Maine (four 12-pound Napoleons), and Ames' Battery G, 1st New York (six 12-pound Napoleons). O.R. Vol. 27.1, p. 238. Hunt did not state where Cooper's guns were positioned among these batteries once they arrived. Today, the positions of these batteries are marked along South Hancock Avenue south of the Pennsylvania Memorial.

100 Hess, p. 117. But this figure also assumes that McGilvery had 39 guns rather than 33. Estimates on the total number of Federal guns also vary. Compare: Coddington, p. 497. His figure is 118.

101 From Herb S. Crumb, ed., The Eleventh Corps Artillery at Gettysburg: The Papers of Major Thomas Osborn, Chief of Artillery (Hamilton: New York: Edmonston Publishing, Inc., 1991), p. 34. Used by permission of the publisher.

102 Ibid.

[103] Hess, p. 145-149.

[104] Nicholson, p. 882. Gardner said that the battery came to Cemetery Ridge along a lane northwest of what was referred to as Granite Knob. See Gardner's letter to Colonel John P. Nicholson dated October 22, 1902, GNMPL. Probably the "Granite Knob" is the knoll where the New Jersey Brigade monument is located today. There was a lane extending west from the Taneytown Road near where the Reserve Artillery was located. It went past the George Weikert home slightly north of where current-day United States Avenue intersects Hancock Avenue. The present-day marker for placement of Cooper's guns on Cemetery Ridge incorrectly recites that Cooper's battery arrived there from East Cemetery Hill. The battery had been parked in reserve after leaving East Cemetery Hill on the prior evening.

According to one member of the battery, the time was about 3:00 p.m. Diary of John W. Alloway, Battery B Papers, Brake Collection, U.S. Army Military History Institute, Ridgway Hall, Carlisle, PA. Alloway's diary is also found in GNMPL; See also O.R. Vol. 27.1, p. 365. But there are conflicting accounts of how long the cannonade lasted. One author estimated that it ended about 2:00 p.m. Hess, pp. 162-163. George R. Stewart in his classic Pickett's Charge, cited several accounts and suggested that it ended close to 3:00 p.m. Stewart, Pickett's Charge, (Boston: Houghton Mifflin Co., 1959), p. 159. The actual time has relevance to James A. Gardner's account. If the cannonade lasted until 2:00 p.m. and assuming that the battery did not get into position until 3:00 p.m., then Gardner could not have witnessed the fire at its height, unless the battery was there earlier. If, however, the firing lasted until 3:00 p.m. when the battery arrived, it is possible that Gardner accurately described the scene. General Hunt's report stated that Cooper's battery was added to the other guns on McGilvery's line "soon after the cannonade commenced." O.R. Vol. 27.1, p. 238. Therefore, it is also possible that the battery was there earlier than 2:00 p.m.

[105] Nicholson, pp. 882-883; O.R. Vol. 27.1, p. 365. There was a suggestion that the relieved battery was that of Captain James Rorty's Battery B, 1st New York. Ladd & Ladd, Vol. 3, p. 1630, ft. nt. 55. That battery was located further up Cemetery Ridge, the monument today being well north of the marker for Cooper's position. Also that battery was involved in the fighting with Pickett's men during the climax of the attack so it could have hardly been replaced before then. James A. Gardner was uncertain of the identity of the battery that was relieved. Ladd & Ladd, Vol. 3, p. 1630. Captain A. Judson Clark's Battery B, First New Jersey was in position among McGilvery's batteries but was not engaged. O.R. 27.1, p. 586; See marker to Clark's battery on Cemetery Ridge. Possibly, it was his battery that was thought to be relieved.

After the war, Gardner felt that the position of Cooper's battery was not marked correctly. He suggested that the battery was actually located further south, between Dow's 6th Maine Battery and Sterling's 2nd Connecticut in the position where the 2nd Connecticut monument was placed and extending north a distance of 100 feet. See Gardner's letter to Colonel John P. Nicholson dated October 22, 1902, GNMPL. Earlier, Gardner stated that the right gun of the battery was in front of where a cavalry monument was being erected in the rear of the battery's position. See Gardner's letter to Colonel Bachelder dated September 20, 1889 in Ladd & Ladd, Vol. 3, pp. 1630-1631. This might probably be the 4th PA Cavalry monument which is further north along Hancock Avenue but yet not close to the current marker for Cooper's battery. It is also in the vicinity where the present marker for Clark's battery is located.

One author has suggested that Cooper's guns were between Sterling's guns and Rank's section of the 3rd Pennsylvania Artillery where the present marker to Clark's battery is located. See: David Shultz, "Double Canister at Ten Yards" (Redondo Beach, California: Rank and File Publications, 1995), p. 45. In making this conclusion, Shultz reversed Rank's and Sterling's positions from the order mentioned by Hunt in his report. See also: Rich Rollins and David Shultz, Guide to Pennsylvania Troops at Gettysburg, (Redondo Beach, California: Rank and File Publications, 1996), p. 164. Notwithstanding that reversal, Shultz's placement more closely coincides with Gardner's recollection to Bachelder. Jeffry D. Wert also placed Cooper's battery further south along Cemetery Ridge between Rank's and Dow's batteries (using Hunt's position order). Jeffry D. Wert, Gettysburg, Day Three, (New York: Simon & Schuster, 2001), p. 142. One thing is certain from all these sources: Cooper's battery was not located on Cemetery Ridge where it is presently marked.

Shultz also stated that Cooper opened on a Confederate battery and sent a round into a barn, setting it on fire. Shultz "Double Canister...," p. 46. While Shultz cites Cooper's report for this incident, the only reference in the actual report by Cooper is that his guns "...immediately opened upon a shattered battery of the enemy which was firing on our front." O.R. Vol. 27.1, p. 365. There is no mention of the burning of a barn in Cooper's report. (Actually, of all the reports of the battery commanders cited by Shultz, only one, that of Captain Patrick Hart, mentions a burning barn which he stated was burned after his guns blew up an enemy caisson nearby. This took place after the charge was repulsed. See O.R. Vol. 27.1, p. 888). Shultz further suggested that after the repulse of the Confederate attack, a Confederate battery that had moved into the position northeast of the burning Klingle barn was destroyed by the combined fire of many Federal batteries, including Cooper's. He indicated that the reports of all the battery commanders related this incident in their post battle reports. Shultz, "Double Canister...," p. 64.

As far as Cooper's report is concerned, any reference to destroying a Confederate battery occurred with his opening on a shattered enemy battery when it first got into position and not after the repulse. O.R. Vol. 27.1, p. 365. James A Gardner, however, claimed that Cooper's guns shattered a battery of the Washington Artillery (Major Benjamin Eshelman's) that had moved out in support of Pickett and forced it to withdraw. Nicholson, p. 883. Captain Jabez Daniels mentioned disabling a Confederate battery before the charge. O.R. Vol. 27.1, p. 1023. Lieutenant Augustus Parsons stated that his battery fired upon an enemy battery after the charge but did not disable it. O.R. Vol. 27.1, p. 900. Only Captain Charles A. Phillips reported driving off a rebel battery by the fire of the First Brigade Artillery after the charge. O.R. Vol. 27.1, p. 885. Neither Captain Nelson Ames nor Lieutenant William Wheeler mentioned anything about silencing a Confederate battery or the burning of a barn. O.R. Vol. 27.1, pp. 901, 753. No report of Lieutenant Evan Thomas was found in the Official Records by this author.

[106] James A. Gardner stated that Cooper's battery fired into the right flank of Pickett. Nicholson, p. 883. Shultz stated that Cooper's battery got into position too late to engage the right flank of Pickett's division. Shultz, p. 45.

[107] O.R. Vol. 27.1, p. 365; Nicholson, p. 883.

[108] George Clark, "Wilcox's Alabama Brigade at Gettysburg," Confederate Veteran, Vol. 17 (1909): 230. In all probability, the "scrubby timbered drain" was the Plum Run line to the west of Cooper's position.

[109] Hess, pp. 305-306.

[110] Nicholson, p. 883.

[111] Casualty List for July 3, 1863, Ibid.; O.R. Vol. 27.1, p. 365; Nicholson, Ibid. The total casualties over three days were 3 killed and 9 wounded out of 106 men engaged, a rate of 11.3% loss. John W. Busey and David G. Martin, Regimental Strengths and Losses at Gettysburg (Hightstown, New Jersey: Longstreet House, 1986), p. 241. But Busey and Martin failed to include James Alcorn as one of the battery's members who was captured on July 1.

[112] O.R. Vol. 27.1, p. 365; Nicholson, p. 883

[113] This account of James P. Alcorn is taken from the Recollections of James P. Alcorn, Ibid., GNMPL. The reader is advised that Alcorn wrote this about 25 years after the battle. But while he admitted that his recollection might have been impaired somewhat by that lapse of time, the events had made such an impression that, in Alcorn's words, "...they rise before me in all the vividness of the occurrences of yesterday." The transcript of his recollections was provided by Ada Marie Bowers, a descendent of the Alcorn family.

[114] Alcorn's Recollections, Ibid. Approximately1,500 prisoners of the First Corps were paroled on the field by Confederate officers. While General Lee proposed an exchange of prisoners, General Meade did not acquiesce. There were several directives that suggested that the Federal government would not honor paroles, and so anyone paroled on the field and sent into Federal lines at Carlisle could still be returned into their regiments or batteries. Gregory A. Coco, A Strange and Blighted Land, Gettysburg: The Aftermath of a Battle (Gettysburg: Thomas Publications,1995), pp. 257-259; Coddington, p. 541. If the prisoners did not accept parole, they would be marched to southern prisons. On the other hand, if they did but the Federal government did not recognize the parole and sent the soldier back into the army, then, theoretically, that soldier was subject to execution if captured. According to the rules of warfare, parolees could only return once exchanged for an enemy parolee or captive. Needless to say, these rules were not consistently followed. Also some soldiers deliberately sought capture so that they could be paroled and leave the fighting. Since the North had greater manpower anyway, there was no real incentive to return captured Confederates back into the ranks. All of this made the parole system fall apart later in the war.

[115] But one source indicated that before leaving for Carlisle, the prisoners were supplied with two days rations. Coco, A Strange and Blighted Land, p. 259.

[116] Alcorn's Recollections, Ibid.

[117] Ibid.

[118] Ibid.

[119] Papertown is present-day Mount Holly Springs.

[120] Alcorn's Recollections, Ibid. About eleven 14th Brooklyn Zouaves had been paroled and placed under the control of a Georgia regiment while proceeding to Carlisle. Coco, A Strange and Blighted Land, p. 259.

[121] Alcorn's Recollections, Ibid.

[122] Ibid.

[123] Actually, the parolees were transported to a parole camp in Westchester, Pennsylvania. Coco, A Strange and Blighted Land, p. 259.

[124] Alcorn's Recollections, Ibid.

[125] Ibid.

[126] Ibid.

[127] This can be corroborated somewhat by a period photograph of Confederate prisoners after the battle which was taken on Seminary Ridge near the Krauth House. A pile of rails made into a barricade can be seen with the three prisoners alongside. Frassanito, Gettysburg, A Journey in Time, pp. 70-71. James stated that he and his brother were at Dr. Croft's house which was used as a field hospital. As mentioned previously, James apparently mistook the name Croft for Krauth.

[128] Alcorn's Recollections, Ibid.

[129] Ibid.

[130] Ibid. This fanciful part of his recollection is incorrect because Alcorn did not actually enter service in April; and while he referred to himself as being 19, he was born on May 28,1840, which would have made him older. See: Obituary, Kinsley Graphic, Ibid. Gravestone at Hillside Cemetery, Kinsley, Kansas (B-5-17). The unit roster in Bates, History of the Pennsylvania Volunteers, Vol. 1, has the date of muster as June 28, 1861.

[131] Obituary, Kinsley Graphic, Ibid.

[132] Ibid.

[133] Ibid. See meeting notes of Battery B Memorial Association on June 8, 1911. Battery B Reunion Memorabilia, Manuscript Group 18, The PA State Archives, Harrisburg, PA.

[134] Obituary, Kinsley Graphic, Ibid. The Grand Army of the Republic (GAR) was an organization comprised of former union soldiers and consisted of individual posts throughout the country.

[135] Battery B Reunion Memorabilia, Ibid. See also: Mount Jackson Sesquicentennial 1815-1965, ([n.p.] 1965), p. 64, for June 8, 1869 as the date for the first reunion.

[136] Battery B Reunion Memorabilia, Ibid.; Mount Jackson Sesquicentennial 1815-1965, p. 65.

[137] Mount Jackson Sesquicentennial 1815-1965, Ibid. The local band was the Mount Jackson Orchestra. Battery B. Reunion Memorabilia, Ibid.

[138] Gettysburg Archives, Box 10, Folder 18, Gett. 4141, GNMP. That marker is still in place today, although the inscription is illegible due to weathering over the years. See also: Newton, Silent Sentinels, pp. 108-109 for the inscription based on that author's research in which J. Howard Wert, A Complete Handbook of the Monuments and Indications and Guide to the Positions on the Gettysburg Battlefield (Harrisburg: R,M. Sturgeon & Co., 1886), p. 185 is cited.

[139] Agreement, GNMPL. The members of that committee were former members of the battery and included Cooper, James A. Gardner, William McClelland, John Q. Stewart, and Isaac A. Nesbit. The cost was paid from an appropriation by the Commonwealth of Pennsylvania supplemented by individual contributions mostly from members of the Battery B Memorial Association.

[140] Mount. Jackson Sesquicentennial 1815-1965, p. 65. A monument fund had been created for this purpose. At the June 8, 1911, reunion meeting there were $1,100.00 in subscriptions of which $700.00 had been paid. Battery B Reunion Memorabilia, Ibid.

[141] See Agreement recorded in Register's and Recorder's Office of Lawrence County Government Center, New Castle, PA in Agreement Book Volume 15, Page 390, recorded on June 3, 1912.

[142] Mount Jackson Sesquicentennial 1815-1965, p. 65.

[143] Battery B Reunion Memorabilia, Ibid.

[144] Subscription request by Charles Weitz, Treasurer, Bessemer Bank, Bessemer, PA, GNMPL.

[145] Gettysburg Archives, Box 10, Folder 19, Gett. 4141, GNMP. The marker was purchased entirely with money raised by Lawrence County citizens and was made of light Barre granite, erected by the Oak Park Monument Company of New Castle, which was owned by C. Wayne Cannon. See also: New Castle News, July 27, 1943.

[146] Aaron L. Hazen, 20th Century History of New Castle & Lawrence County (Chicago: Richmond Arnold Publishing Co.,1908), pp. 400-401; Copy of discharge at Lawrence County Government Center, New Castle, PA, Discharge Book Volume 10, page 62; Obituary, New Castle News, May 25, 1925; Lawrence Co. Bar Assn. Memorial at No. 15, p. 26, Misc. Docket, Lawrence County Government Center, New Castle, PA. See Gardner's correspondence on file at GNMPL.

[147] Battery B Reunion Memorabilia, Ibid.

[148] Lieutenant William C. Miller took command until he mustered out on November 22, 1864. William McClelland became captain and continued in command until the unit mustered out on June 9, 1865. Bates, History of the Pennsylvania Volunteers, Vol. 1, pp. 952, 976.

[149] Mortgage of Captain J. Harvey Cooper to James H. Cameron 1866; Receipts from Hammond & Cooper Lumber Co., 1867; U.S. Internal Revenue Return for Special Tax, 1868. The receipts of the lumber company were pre-printed in the name of Hammond & Cameron with the latter's name crossed out and "Cooper" written in its place. Manuscript Group 18, The PA State Archives, Harrisburg, PA. This suggests that perhaps the mortgage, in the amount of $3,200, was to purchase Cameron's interest in the business.

[150] Obituary, "Captain J.H. Cooper Honored Citizen and Brave Soldier Dies," New Castle Herald, March 21, 1906, p. 1; Obituary, "Captain J.H. Cooper Answered the Last Call this Morning, "New Castle News, March 21, 1906, p. 1.

[151] Nicholson, pp. 885-886.

SOME UNANSWERED QUESTIONS

One of the mysteries in the action of the battery on July 2, was to whom Colonel Wainwright was referring when he described the death of two artillerymen during the Cooper's duel with Latimer's battery on Benner's Hill. In his journal, Wainwright described sitting on the stone wall between Cooper's guns and those of Captain Michael Wiedrich on East Cemetery Hill, accompanied by General Adelbert Ames of the Eleventh Corps, and witnessing the effect of the rounds fired from Benner's Hill. With reference to the one nearly annihilating the crew of one of Cooper's guns, he stated:

The other was a shell which burst directly under Cooper's left gun, killed one man outright, blew another all to pieces, so that he died in half an hour, and wounded the other three....The man who was so badly blown to pieces lost his right hand, his left arm at the shoulder, and his ribs so broken that you could see right into him; he was removed to the well, just inside the cemetery gates, and died there. Cooper came to me and asked permission for his brother, who was their bugler, to go and remain with him while he lived....[1]

The battery's casualties for July 2 listed two men, Privates James H. McCleary and Peter G. Hoagland, who were killed. Private Jesse Temple was wounded severely while Privates J.C. Cornelius, D.W. Taylor, and Corporal Joseph Reed were wounded slightly.[2] A perusal of the roster for the unit as found in Bates' History of the Pennsylvania Volunteers, shows only one individual having a similar surname to one of the two who were killed. That individual is Corporal Lee S. McCleary who was also at Gettysburg. But he was not listed as a bugler.[3] Nor was he a brother of James McCleary. There is no other person listed with the surname of Hoagland. Harry W. Pfanz in his book Gettysburg, Culp's Hill & Cemetery Hill noted that he had not been able to identify the brothers referred to by Wainwright.[4] Gregory A. Coco in his book Killed in Action was willing to be more speculative and suggested that the artilleryman who died behind the cemetery gatehouse was very likely James McCleary.[5]

James McCleary was the eldest son of William and Selinda McCleary of Little Beaver Township, Lawrence County, Pennsylvania. The 1860 census shows that the William McCleary family had nine children with only James and his brother John being males of sufficient age to serve in the military once the war began.[6] A record of the men of Lawrence County serving during the war shows a John C. McCleary from Little Beaver Township who enlisted in the 134th Pennsylvania Infantry on August 19, 1862, and was discharged from that unit on May 26, 1863. His rank was listed as first sergeant of Co. I.[7]

Lee S. McCleary (whose given name was Leander Sample McCleary) died in 1876 at age 41.[8] His father was Samuel McCleary.[9] While Lee might have been related to James in some fashion, the evidence does not demonstrate that he was James' brother. Just based on the names listed in Bates' compilation as

Lee Sample McCleary who was at Gettysburg but was not the brother of James H. McCleary, the latter being mortally wounded on July 2. (Courtesy of Kenneth C. Turner)

well as those on the bronze plaque on the Pennsylvania Memorial at Gettysburg, there was no one else who, conceivably, could be a brother of James McCleary once Lee S. McCleary is eliminated from consideration.

The place and date of death along with the reported injuries of the men who were killed further compound the puzzle. Keeping in mind that Wainwright stated that one man was killed outright and the other died about a half hour later behind the cemetery gate from injuries to the hand, arm and broken ribs, one source has suggested that neither McCleary nor Hoagland were killed immediately nor did either one die at the cemetery gate. According to that source, both men died at the Artillery Brigade First Corps Hospital, McCleary dying on July 2 and Hoagland on July 4.[10] The hospital as of July 2 was located in the area of White Church and the Isaac Lightner farm off the Baltimore Pike, being a distance south of the cemetery gate.[11]

Also, the mortal injuries sustained by McCleary were reported to involve both legs which were amputated.[12] Coco in Killed in Action, recognized that McCleary had these injuries, but suggested that they were in addition to those mentioned by Wainwright.[13] A moment's reflection, however, compels the inference that given the specificity of the injuries described by Wainwright of the artilleryman who was so "badly blown to pieces," it is doubtful that he would have neglected to see the injuries to both legs at the same time. It is also doubtful that surgeons would have taken the time to amputate both legs at a field hospital if the other wounds as Wainwright had described were so apparently mortal in themselves.

As mentioned above, Hoagland did not die until July 4, so he hardly could have been either the individual killed outright or who died within a half hour of his wounding on July 2. He was initially buried at the George Spangler farm between the Taneytown Road and Baltimore Pike, south of Granite Schoolhouse Road. Later, he was moved to the German Reformed Church Cemetery until July 5, 1901, when he was disinterred and reburied in the Soldiers' National Cemetery.[14]

Just who the men were that Wainwright described is an enigma. Neither of the two artillerymen, McCleary nor Hoagland, quite fit with Wainwright's description when considering other circumstances surrounding their death. This is so even though they were the only ones from the battery who were killed or died from wounds received on July 2. The mystery, at least from this perspective, is still unresolved.

Notes

[1]   Nevins, p. 243. Wainwright refers to this incident briefly in his battle report of July 17, 1863. O.R. Vol. 27.1, p. 358.

[2]   O.R. Vol. 27.1, p. 365; See also Nicholson, p. 882.

[3]   Bates, History of the Pennsylvania Volunteers, Vol. 1, pp. 976-983. The battery bugler during the period of Gettysburg is listed as David Witherspoon in the Bates' roster. Lee S. McCleary is also listed on the roster of men in the battery on the bronze tablets of the Pennsylvania Memorial at Gettysburg.

[4]   Pfanz, Gettysburg, Culp's Hill & Cemetery Hill, p. 437, nt. 31.

[5]   Gregory A. Coco, Killed in Action, (Gettysburg: Thomas Publications, 1992), p. 55.

[6]   The Lawrence Journal, July 11, 1863, p. 2 referred to the death of James McCleary at Gettysburg whose father was William McCleary of Little Beaver Township. The 1860 census showed the following entries for the William McCleary family of Little Beaver Township: William, age 48 years; Salinda, age 44 years; James, age 21 years; John, age 19 years; Mary, age 17 years; George, age 12 years; Catherine, age 10 years; William, age 8 years; Elliot, age 6 years; Joseph, age 3 years; and Charles, age 10 months. In the 1850 Census records for the William McCleary family then living in Neshannock Township, Lawrence County, Pennsylvania, William was listed as age 37 years, Salinda as age 34 years, James, age 11 years, John, age

9 years, Mary age 7 years, and George age 2 years. The other children reflected in the 1860 census were not yet born in 1850. In 1865, the McCleary's moved to Dixon, Illinois. William died in November, 1879, and Salinda in 1909. Salinda's obituary listed James as her eldest son who was killed at Gettysburg and referred to her other eight surviving children noted above. See: Obituary, "Death Comes at Easter's Close," The New Castle News, April 15, 1909, p. 8.

[7] 1877 History of Lawrence County, PA (Reprinted, Evansville, Indiana: Unigraphic, Inc., 1976), pp. 218-219.

[8] See: Obituary, Lawrence Guardian, June 24, 1876, p. 3.

[9] Last Will and Testament of Samuel McCleary probated in Lawrence County, Pennsylvania in 1858. There is a specific bequest to Leander Sample McCleary. Will Book Volume 1, page 404.

[10] John W. Busey, The Last Full Measure, pp. 137 and 168.

[11] Coco, A Strange and Blighted Land, p. 193. See also: G. Coco, A Vast Sea of Misery (Gettysburg: Thomas Publications, 1988), pp. 83, 84. There is a battlefield marker at White Church Road and Baltimore Pike stating that on July 2 the First Corps hospitals were established near White Church. But there is one reference suggesting that the gatehouse was used as a hospital because Elizabeth Thorn, the cemetery caretaker's wife, had found six amputated legs in the yard. See Busey, The Last Full Measure, p. xxv.

[12] Busey, The Last Full Measure, p. 168.

[13] Coco, Killed in Action, p. 55. If, as Busey mentioned, there were six amputated legs found near the gatehouse, it is possible that any amputation of McCleary's legs took place there and he later died at the First Corps hospital.

[14] Pennsylvania Section, Row G, No. 28. Busey, The Last Full Measure, p. 137; John W. Busey, From These Honored Dead (Hightstown, New Jersey: Longstreet House, 1996), p. 304. McCleary and Alcorn were interred in the Evergreen Cemetery behind the gatehouse in a special plot of 91 soldiers dug by Elizabeth Thorn and her father. Thorn's husband, the caretaker, was absent, and she was six months pregnant at the time. The fee was $2.50 each, and the burials began on July 6. Busey, The Last Full Measure, pp. 163-164. The spot, known as Area C of the Evergreen Cemetery today, has individual grave markers listing the names and units of soldiers buried there. McCleary and Alcorn are among those so identified.

CONCLUSION

Cooper's Battery, along with the other guns of Colonel Wainwright's artillery brigade, performed very well, particularly on the first day, when they exhibited flexibility and teamwork by occupying different portions of the field to go where they were needed. It was equally obvious that Federal infantry commanders still did not fully appreciate the advantages of having an overall officer of the artillery brigade to oversee the placement of the guns. In several instances, they tried to usurp Wainwright's authority on the field.

Cooper's Battery engaged in both counterbattery and close range defensive fire, being especially effective in the former on East Cemetery Hill to help neutralize Latimer's threat from Benner's Hill. Earlier on July 1 his men, with just three operating rifled pieces, acquitted themselves well in helping to stop Scales' attack against the Federal line on Seminary Ridge. Gettysburg was illustrative of the battery's performance throughout the entire conflict. It was a unit that knew its responsibility in difficult situations and could be counted upon to fulfill it.

After the war, the men in the battery tried to perpetuate the memory and sacrifices of their service through annual reunions that occurred on a regular basis in Mount Jackson for over 50 years. The community supported those efforts until the remaining veterans could no longer participate. As time went on, Battery B became a distant memory for many, even with the celebration of the war's centennial in the 1960's.

Pennsylvania Memorial at Gettysburg. Bronze plaques surrounding its base provide rosters of each Pennsylvania unit at the battle.

Mount Jackson today is still basically rural with some small local businesses operating in the area. Jackson Knolls is a housing development located in what was formerly Nesbit's Grove where gatherings for the battery's reunions took place. One of the streets in the development is called Battery B Street. Close by is the small community of Bessemer where the prominent manufacturing activity is a cement plant. There are dairy and produce farms scattered throughout the landscape. In fact, every spring at the local high school, the students whose parents have farms traditionally drive the family tractor to the parking lot of the school on "tractor day." On the road toward Enon Valley from Mount Jackson, one passes the entrance to the SNPJ campsite, an incorporated municipality in itself, which sponsors celebrations of Slovenian music and culture.

People traveling along Route 108 to go to the school, Bessemer, Enon Valley, or the campsite pass the monument to Battery B with the cannon located alongside. Few take the time to notice it. Even fewer appreciate its significance. The Methodist Episcopal Church on top of the hill overlooking it is no longer there.[1] The local elementary school takes its fifth grade class on annual trips to Gettysburg where one of the focal points is a visit to East Cemetery Hill to see the larger monument to the battery. But few visitors from the area realize that two of its local sons, Alexander Alcorn and James McCleary, are buried in marked graves just behind the gatehouse to the rear of that monument. Still others do not know that Peter Hoagland is buried in the Soldier's National Cemetery or that the battery as a whole reputedly had the most

1ST ARTILLERY
FORTY-THIRD REGIMENT FOURTEENTH RESERVE

COOPERS BATTERY B

CAPTAIN JAMES H COOPER
1ST LT ISAAC A NESBIT
2ND LT WILLIAM C MILLER

SERGEANTS	PRIVATES			
JOHN M FULLERTON	ALEX P ALCORN	QUINTON A DUNGAN	WILLIAM LUSK	THOMAS H REED
HIRAM EVANS	DAVID B AUGUS	WILLIAM DAVIS	SAMUEL J LANE	JOHN REED
JAMES P ALCORN	JOHN W ALLEN	WILLIAM H H DAVIS	JEREMIAH LYSHEON	ABRAM RHODES
SAMUEL DUNNAN	JOHN W ALLOWAY	CYRUS W DAVIS	JOHN MELLIES	THOMAS C RICE
JOHN G HAMILL	GEORGE BENDER	WM W EICHBAUM	DAVID H McCLUSKEY	J D SHINGLEDECKER
	JOSEPH BUCHANAN	EPHRAIM K C EVANS	JOHN A MENOR	GOBESKI A SHAFFER
CORPORALS	DAVID BARGE	GEORGE W FERRELL	JAMES A McCREADY	ASEL SHAFFER
WILLIAM W OFFICER	JOHN A CRAIG	JOHN FERGUSON	JAMES H McCLEARY	THOMAS M SWISHER
ALFRED M SWISHER	JOHN L CAMBLIN	JOHN H GEALY	JACOB N MYERS	ROBERT P STEEN
JOSEPH REED	WILLIAM CHAMBERS	JAMES A GARDNER	DAVID MANLEY	JOHN W SUMMERS
SAMUEL K McGINNIS	JAMES C CORNELIUS	JEFFERSON GRUBB	J P MONASMITH	DANIEL W TAYLOR
JAMES H MACLAY	JOHN W CORLE	GEORGE C GARBER	JOSEPH MANLEY	PERSIFER TAYLOR
LEE S McCLEARY	ROBERT CRAVEN	SAMUEL HANNA	WILLIAM MYERS	JESSE TEMPLE
THOMAS BRAYDEN	JAMES B COVERT	PETER G HOAGLAND	GEO J McGINNIS	DAVID M WESTON
JOHN T CRAMER	JOHN DUNNAN	J A HEASLEY	DAVID P NEEDLER	JOHN A WESTON
		FRANCIS M HOOVER	GEORGE W PITZER	THOMAS W WELLAR
		JAMES R HOPE	JOHN W PHILLIPS	DAVID WITHERSPOON
		FREDERICK KOERNER	MARTIN PYLE	FREDERICK WORKMAN
		JAMES C KINCAID	JOHN PAULY	SAMUEL L WHITE
		JOHN KIRKWOOD	WILLIAM ROWLAND	JACOB WISE
		SAMUEL KING	JAMES S ROWLAND	

RICKETTS BATTERY F & G

BATTERY F

CAPTAIN R BRUCE RICKETTS

	DANIEL BUBB	SAMUEL HILING	JOHN G RAKE
	CHARLES H CLARK	JOHN F HINMAN	JAMES H RIGGIN
	WILLIAM COULTER	SAMUEL KYLER	CHARLES SHIPNER

Bronze plaque at the base of the Pennsylvania Memorial showing the names of the men of the battery at Gettysburg.

battle deaths of any Federal voluntary light artillery unit in the entire war.[2] For the most part, the Civil War and the memory of Battery B have been submerged in the psyche of the people as they go about their everyday lives and occupations. This is understandable and inevitable.

No one today can truly appreciate the sense of community pride that existed in 1869 when the veterans were honored in the first of many annual reunions or when the local monument was dedicated in 1912. There are no parades or speeches commemorating Battery B's service anymore. No politicians extol the sacrifices the men of the battery or memorialize those who died fighting for the sake of a unified country. Few living today can even recall that in the 1940's while this country was in the midst of a world conflict, the citizenry was able to obtain enough funds to have a marker erected honoring the battery's contributions on the first day's field of battle. The monuments are certainly there for us to see if we care to look, and the story can be told again so we do not forget. But do we really see and listen? After all, it was a long time ago. Hopefully, the story told here will serve as a reminder of the spirit and dedication of a group of young men from a small rural community who, in brotherhood together, wrote their own page in the annals of American history. It was a record of which we can all be proud.

Notes

---

[1] The church, built in 1842, was destroyed by fire on July 26, 1915. "Mt. Jackson Church Goes Up in Smoke," New Castle News, July 26, 1915; Mt. Jackson Sesquicentennial 1815-1965, p. 16.

[2] Nicholson, p. 885.

48

MEMBERS OF COOPER'S BATTERY B AT GETTYSBURG[1]

CAPTAIN JAMES H. COOPER
FIRST LIEUTENANT ISAAC A. NESBIT
SECOND LIEUTENANT WILLIAM C. MILLER [w]

Sergeants:

John M. Fullerton
Hiram Evans
James P. Alcorn[2]
Samuel Dunnan
John S. Hamill

Corporals:

William W. Officer
Alfred M. Swisher
Joseph Reed [w]
Samuel K. McGinnis
James H. Maclay

Lee S. McCleary
Thomas Brayden
John T. Cramer [Creamer]

Privates:

Alex P. Alcorn (k)
David B. Angus
John W. Allen
John W. Alloway
George Bender
Joseph Buchanan
David Barge
John A. Craig
John L. Camblin
William Chambers
James C. Cornelius [w]
John W. Corle [Corl]
Robert Craven
James B. Covert
John Dunnan
Quinton A. Dungan
William Davis
William H. H. Davis
Cyrus W. Davis
Wm. W. Eichbaum
Ephraim K. C. Evans
George W. Ferrell [Ferrel]
John Ferguson
John H. Gealy
James A. Gardner
Jefferson [Isaac J.] Grubb
George C. Garber

Samuel Hanna
Peter G. Hoagland (k)
J. [John] A. Heasley
Francis M. Hoover
James R. Hope
Frederick Koerner
James C. Kincaid [Kincade]
John Kirkwood
Samuel King
William Lusk
Samuel J. Lane
Jeremiah Lysheon
John Mellies [Milleis]
David H. McCluskey
John A. Menor [Meanor]
James A. McCready
James H. McCleary (k)
Jacob N. Myers
David Manley
J. [Jno.] P. Monasmith
Joseph Manley
William Myers
Geo. J. McGinnis
David P. Needler
George W. Pitzer
John W. Phillips [w]
Martin Pyle

John Pauly [w]
William [C.] Rowland
[Roland]
James S. Rowland [Roland]
Thomas H. Reed
John Reed
Abram Rhodes [Rhoades]
Thomas C. Rice
J. D. [J. B.] Shingledecker
Sobeski A. Shaffer
Asel [Asahel] Shaffer [w]
Thomas M. Swisher
Robert P. Steen
John W. Summers
Daniel W. Taylor [w]
Persifer Taylor
Jesse Temple [w]
David M. Weston
John A. Weston
Thomas W. Wellar
David Witherspoon
Frederick Workman [w]
Samuel L. White
Jacob [N.] Wise

Notes

[1] The names are taken from the roster of the unit at the base of the Pennsylvania Memorial at Gettysburg. Information in brackets is taken from the roster found in Samuel P. Bates' History of the Pennsylvania Volunteers.

[2] Alcorn was captured on July 1 but is not so listed in the Bates' roster.

Battery B, 1st Penna Light Artillery. -Captain James H. Cooper.
In front of Petersburg.

Cooper's Battery in front of Petersburg, Virginia in 1864. Cooper is standing in the foreground leaning on his sword while James A. Gardner is seated on the trail of the first gun on the left in the act of sighting it.
(Photograph from the Massachusetts Military Order of the Loyal Legion of the United States (MOLLUS) Photographic Collection, U.S. Army Military History Institute, Carlisle, Pennsylvania)

Another view of Cooper's Battery in front of Petersburg, Virginia in 1864. Cooper is again leaning on his sword between the first two guns from the left. Famous Civil War photographer, Matthew Brady, dressed in civilian clothes and straw hat, is behind Cooper.
(Photograph from the Massachusetts Military Order of the Loyal Legion of the United States (MOLLUS) Photographic Collection, U.S. Army Military History Institute, Carlisle, Pennsylvania)

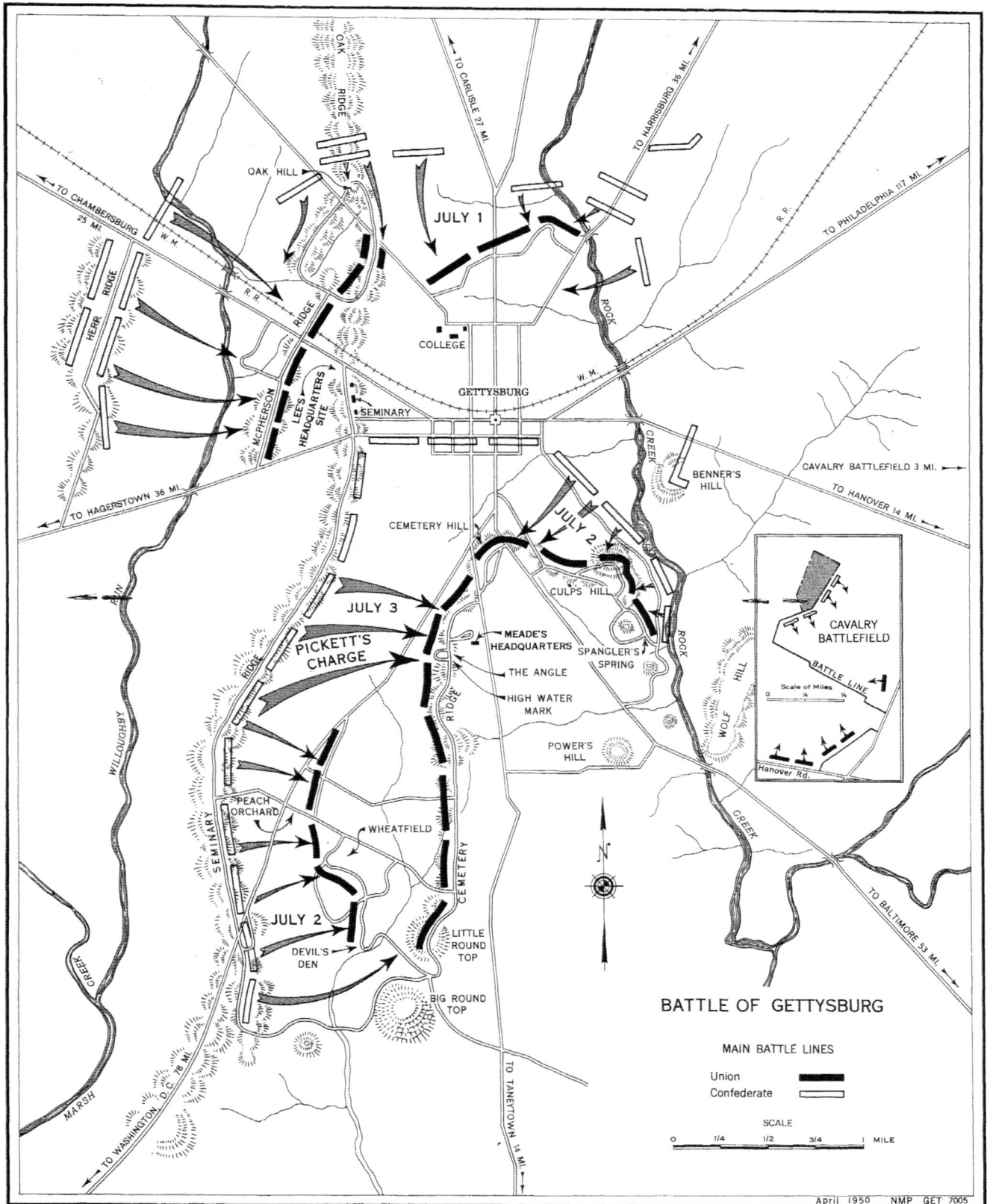

MAIN BATTLE LINES

Union

Confederate

SCALE

0   1/4   1/2   3/4   1 MILE

BATTLE OF GETTYSBURG

Map from Gettysburg National Military Park Historical Handbook Series No. 9